Escaping the Chains of a Toxic Marriage

KAVITA JAISWAL

BLUEROSE PUBLISHERS
India | U.K.

Copyright © Kavita Jaiswal 2024

All rights reserved by author. No part of this publication may be reproduced, stored in a retrieval system or transmitted in any form or by any means, electronic, mechanical, photocopying, recording or otherwise, without the prior permission of the author. Although every precaution has been taken to verify the accuracy of the information contained herein, the publisher assumes no responsibility for any errors or omissions. No liability is assumed for damages that may result from the use of information contained within.

BlueRose Publishers takes no responsibility for any damages, losses, or liabilities that may arise from the use or misuse of the information, products, or services provided in this publication.

For permissions requests or inquiries regarding this publication, please contact:

BLUEROSE PUBLISHERS
www.BlueRoseONE.com
info@bluerosepublishers.com
+91 8882 898 898
+4407342408967

ISBN: 978-93-6452-778-1

Cover Design: Sadhna Kumari
Typesetting: Pooja Sharma

First Edition: October 2024

Dedicated To,

To those who have endured the silent suffering of lost love, understanding, and empathy in their marriages—this book is for you! I dedicate these pages to the countless hearts weighed down by the darkness of despair, yet brave enough to seek the light. May "Escaping the Chains of Toxic Marriage" offer you not only solace but a path to rediscover your strength, self-worth, and the hope of a brighter tomorrow. You are not alone, and there is life—and love—beyond the shadows.

Foreword

In a world where the sanctity of marriage is often held above all else, it takes unparalleled courage to confront the stark reality that not all unions are sanctuaries of love and respect. Ms. Kavita Jaiswal's profound and compelling work, *Escaping the Chains of Toxic Marriage: The Ultimate Guide to Moving On from a Toxic Marriage*, dares to challenge the deeply entrenched societal norms that bind individuals to relationships that are not only unfulfilling but also destructive. This book is not merely a guide; it is a beacon of hope, a road-map for those ensnared in the dark and suffocating grasp of a toxic marriage.

Ms. Jaiswal's initiative in addressing this pervasive yet often unspoken issue is both timely and necessary. In today's society, where the pressures to maintain a facade of marital bliss can be overwhelming, her work shines a light on the hidden suffering that countless individuals endure behind closed doors. Her insight into the intricacies of toxic relationships is not only profound but also deeply empathetic, offering readers a sense of validation and understanding that is so often lacking in discussions of marital discord.

The relevance of this book cannot be overstated. As Ms. Jaiswal aptly observes, "Toxicity is not just about occasional disagreements or arguments. Every relationship has its share of conflicts—that's a normal part of human interaction. Toxicity, however, refers to a persistent pattern of harmful behaviours, attitudes, and actions that degrade or harm one or both partners." In these words, she encapsulates the essence of what sets a toxic marriage apart from the everyday challenges that all couples face. It is this understanding that forms the foundation of her book—a recognition that the insidious nature of toxicity in marriage is a problem that must be addressed with urgency and compassion.

Ms. Jaiswal's exploration of the psychological, emotional, and social ramifications of toxic marriages is nothing short of masterful. She delves into the devastating impact that such relationships can have on an individual's self-esteem, mental health, and overall well-being. In one particularly poignant passage, she writes, "Living in a toxic marriage feels like you're drowning, suffocating under the weight of constant negativity. The toll it takes is profound, affecting every aspect of your being." These words resonate with the weight of lived experience, offering a glimpse into the soul-crushing despair that so many feel yet cannot articulate.

Yet, what makes *Escaping the Chains of Toxic Marriage* truly remarkable is not just its diagnosis of the problem but its focus on solutions. Ms. Jaiswal does not merely leave her readers in the abyss; she provides them with the tools and guidance needed to climb out and reclaim their lives. Her emphasis on self-worth, empowerment, and the necessity of taking decisive action is a lifeline to those who may feel trapped and hopeless. She reminds us that "Choosing to leave a toxic marriage is not an admission of defeat; it is a courageous step towards a healthier, more fulfilling life." In this, she not only empowers her readers but also reframes the narrative around divorce and separation, challenging the stigma that so often accompanies these decisions.

Moreover, Ms. Jaiswal's work is imbued with a sense of purpose that goes beyond individual healing. She understands that the impact of toxic marriages extends far beyond the couple involved, affecting children, extended family, and even society at large. Her call to action is not just for those trapped in toxic relationships but for all of us to recognize the importance of supporting one another in the pursuit of healthy, respectful, and loving relationships. She writes with a sense of urgency and clarity, making it clear that this is not just a personal issue but a societal one that demands our attention.

In *Escaping the Chains of Toxic Marriage*, Ms. Jaiswal also confronts the societal perceptions that often keep individuals shackled to unhealthy relationships. She challenges the deeply ingrained beliefs that equate marital endurance with success, arguing instead that true success lies in the ability to prioritize one's well-being and happiness. "When society views divorce as a failure rather than a courageous step towards self-preservation, it perpetuates the suffering of countless individuals trapped in toxic relationships," she asserts. This bold stance is both refreshing and necessary, as it calls on society to reevaluate its values and to support those who make the difficult decision to prioritize their mental and emotional health.

It is also worth noting Ms. Jaiswal's exceptional ability to communicate complex psychological and emotional concepts in a manner that is both accessible and engaging. Her writing is clear and concise, yet it is also rich with insight and empathy. She does not shy away from the harsh realities of toxic marriages, but neither does she succumb to despair. Instead, she offers a balanced perspective that acknowledges the pain while also providing hope for healing and renewal.

Ms. Jaiswal's work is a testament to her deep understanding of the human condition and her unwavering commitment to helping others navigate the tumultuous waters of toxic relationships. Her book is a powerful tool for anyone who finds themselves trapped in a toxic marriage, offering not just guidance but also solace and encouragement. It is a work that will undoubtedly have a lasting impact on the lives of its readers, helping them to break free from the chains that bind them and to step into a future filled with possibility and hope.

Escaping the Chains of Toxic Marriage is a book of immense relevance and importance. Ms. Kavita Jaiswal's initiative in writing this guide is a commendable and courageous act, one that addresses a pressing issue in today's society with both sensitivity and insight. Her work is a beacon of light for those navigating the dark and treacherous waters of toxic marriages, offering not just a way out but a path toward a life of freedom, dignity, and fulfilment. This book is a must-read for anyone who has ever questioned their place in a marriage that feels more like a prison than a partnership. Ms. Jaiswal has given the world a gift of profound wisdom and compassion, and for that, we are all deeply grateful.

Bimalanshu Shekhar Mallik

-Former Senior Lecturer in English, St. Xavier's College, Ranchi

-Former Senior English Faculty, Stamford Commercial College, Bangkok

-Former Senior English Faculty, The American School of Bangkok

-Former Principal, Netarhat Residential School, Jharkhand

Contents

Introduction 1

Understanding Toxicity in Marriage 3

The Cycle of Abuse 14

The Psychology of Toxic Relationships 25

Acknowledge, Accept, Act 36

Planning Your Escape 47

The Journey of Healing 59

The Power of Self-Love 70

Finding Happiness After Toxicity 81

Forgiveness and Letting Go 92

Reclaim Your Life 103

Moving Forward: Building Healthy Relationships 113

Empowering Yourself 126

Cultivating Self-Compassion 137

Building a Supportive Community 148

Embracing Your New Life 159

Introduction

Welcome to a journey of self-discovery, empowerment, and liberation. This book is not just another guide; it's an invitation to reclaim your life from the destructive clutches of a toxic marriage. It's a roadmap that will guide you out of the emotional wilderness and into a landscape of hope, strength, and resilience.

Every person deserves to live a life filled with respect, love, and peace. However, when these basic elements are missing from a marriage, it becomes a breeding ground for toxicity. This book is written for those who find themselves in such a predicament, feeling trapped and suffocated, wondering if there's a way out.

"Escaping the Chains of Toxic Marriage" is not just about identifying the signs of a toxic relationship but also providing practical solutions to navigate your way out. It's about understanding that you are not alone, and more importantly, you are not powerless.

The chapters that follow will take you through the process of recognizing the toxicity in your marriage, understanding its impact on your life, and making the difficult but necessary decision to move on. This book will also guide you through the aftermath of a toxic marriage, helping you heal, rebuild, and rediscover the person you once were.

This journey is not an easy one, but it is necessary. It's about breaking the chains that have held you captive and stepping into a life of freedom and fulfillment. It's about choosing yourself, your well-being, and your happiness. It's about understanding that you are worthy of love and respect and that it's never too late to demand them.

As you turn the pages of this book, remember that it's not about blaming or shaming, but about understanding and healing. It's about starting a new chapter in your life, free from toxicity and filled with hope. So, let's embark on this journey together, one step at a time, towards a brighter and healthier future.

Chapter 1:
Understanding Toxicity in Marriage

Defining Toxicity

In our journey to liberate ourselves from the shackles of a toxic marriage, it is essential first to understand what "toxicity" entails. This term has been thrown around so much that it may feel like a buzzword, but it is far from it. Toxicity is real, and it is damaging. It is a poison that slowly seeps into the fabric of a relationship, gradually eroding the foundation of love, respect, and trust until all that's left is a hollow shell of what once was.

Toxicity is not just occasional disagreements or arguments. Every relationship has its share of conflicts - it is a part of human interaction. Instead, toxicity refers to a persistent pattern of harmful behaviors, attitudes, and actions that belittle, degrade, or otherwise harm one or both parties involved. It is about power and control, with one person consistently imposing their will on the other, often using manipulation, guilt, fear or shame.

In a toxic marriage, love is not about mutual respect and understanding. Instead, it is a weapon used to control and manipulate. It is a twisted version of love that is conditional, contingent on obedience or compliance. In such a relationship, one's self-worth is constantly under attack, leaving them feeling inadequate, unloved, and perpetually walking on eggshells.

A toxic relationship can take many forms. It could be blatant, with overt acts of physical or verbal abuse. It could also be subtle, characterized by passive-aggressive behaviors, emotional manipulation, or gaslighting, where a person is made to question their reality. Regardless of its form, the effects are equally devastating, leading to emotional and psychological distress, and in some cases, physical harm.

Toxicity is not a one-time thing; it is a pattern, a cycle that repeats itself. It starts with tension building, followed by an incident, reconciliation, and calm before the tension starts building again. This cycle may occur so frequently that it becomes normalized, making the victim feel trapped in this never-ending loop of emotional turmoil.

The toxicity in a marriage can be so insidious that it's often hard to recognize, especially when you're in the midst of it. You may find yourself justifying your partner's actions, blaming yourself, or even doubting your feelings. But know this - your feelings are valid. If you feel belittled, controlled, manipulated or abused, it's important to acknowledge these feelings and not dismiss them.

Remember, a healthy relationship is built on mutual respect, understanding, and equality. It is about supporting each other's growth and happiness, not stifling it. It is about love that nourishes, not love that drains. If your marriage lacks these elements, it may be toxic.

Defining toxicity is the first step towards breaking free from it. Once you understand what it is, you can begin to recognize its signs in your relationship. This recognition is the first step towards change. It is the first step towards reclaiming your life, your freedom, your happiness. It is the first step towards escaping the chains of a toxic marriage.

Let's not sugarcoat it; recognizing and admitting that your marriage is toxic can be a painful realization. But remember, this pain is temporary, and it is a necessary part of your journey towards healing and liberation. You are not alone in this journey. You are stronger than you think, and you deserve a life free from toxicity.

Recognizing the Signs

Living in a toxic marriage can feel like being trapped in a labyrinth of confusion and despair. It's easy to lose sight of what a healthy relationship should look like when you're constantly navigating a minefield of emotional manipulation, criticism, and control. Recognizing the signs is the first crucial step in reclaiming your life and breaking free from the chains that bind you.

Imagine waking up every day with a sense of dread, unsure of what mood your partner will be in or how you will be treated. This is not normal. A healthy relationship should be a source of comfort and security, not anxiety and fear. If you find yourself walking on eggshells, constantly trying to avoid conflict or appease your partner, it's a clear indication that something is wrong.

Consider the way your partner communicates with you. Are they supportive and understanding, or do they belittle and demean you? Toxic partners often use words as weapons, aiming to undermine your self-esteem and make you feel worthless. They may disguise their insults as jokes or claim they're only trying to help you improve, but the underlying intent is to control and dominate you.

Another red flag is the level of control your partner exerts over your life. Do they dictate who you can see, what you can do, or how you should spend your time? This controlling behavior is not about love or concern; it's about power. A loving partner respects your autonomy and encourages your independence, rather than seeking to isolate and manipulate you.

Pay attention to how your partner reacts when you express your feelings or concerns. Do they listen and try to understand, or do they dismiss your emotions and make you feel guilty for speaking up? Emotional invalidation is a common tactic in toxic relationships, designed to make you doubt your own perceptions and keep you in a state of confusion.

One of the most insidious aspects of a toxic marriage is the cycle of abuse. Your partner may alternate between periods of kindness and episodes of cruelty, making it difficult to identify the true nature of the relationship. This intermittent reinforcement can keep you trapped, always hoping that the good times will return and clinging to the belief that things will get better.

It's also important to recognize the physical signs of stress and anxiety that can result from living in a toxic marriage. Chronic headaches, fatigue, and digestive issues are just a few examples of how your body may be responding to the constant tension and emotional turmoil. Ignoring these symptoms can lead to serious health problems, further trapping you in a cycle of misery.

The realization that you are in a toxic marriage can be both liberating and terrifying. It's natural to feel a mix of emotions, including fear, anger, and sadness. However, acknowledging the reality of your situation is a powerful act of self-love and the first step toward healing. You deserve to be in a relationship where you are valued, respected, and cherished. Recognizing the signs of a toxic marriage is not just about identifying the problem; it's about empowering yourself to take action and reclaim your life.

Effects on the Individual

Imagine waking up every day feeling like you're drowning, suffocating under the weight of a toxic marriage. The toll it takes on an individual is profound, reaching deep into the core of one's being. The emotional scars, while invisible to the naked eye, are as real and painful as any physical wound. Living in such an environment erodes self-esteem, leaving one questioning their worth and abilities. The constant barrage of negativity and manipulation can make even the strongest person feel insignificant and powerless.

The psychological impact is devastating. Anxiety and depression become unwelcome companions, creeping into every aspect of life. The mind is in a perpetual state of alert, always preparing for the next conflict or hurtful comment. Sleep becomes elusive, as worries and fears dominate the night. The once vibrant and hopeful spirit becomes a shadow of its former self, trapped in a cycle of despair and hopelessness.

Physical health is not spared either. The stress and tension manifest in various ailments – headaches, stomach issues, and chronic pain. The body, under constant strain, begins to break down. Immune systems weaken, making one more susceptible to illnesses. The energy to engage in life's simplest pleasures diminishes, replaced by a constant state of fatigue and exhaustion.

Social connections suffer greatly. Friends and family, once sources of joy and support, become distant memories as isolation sets in. The toxic partner's influence often extends to these relationships, creating rifts and misunderstandings. One may feel embarrassed or ashamed to admit the reality of their situation, further deepening the sense of loneliness. The vibrant network of connections that once provided strength and comfort dwindles, leaving a void that seems impossible to fill.

The impact on professional life is equally significant. Concentration and productivity plummet, as the mind is preoccupied with personal turmoil. The workplace, once a sanctuary or a place of achievement, becomes another arena of stress. Career progression stalls, and opportunities are missed, as the energy and focus required to excel are sapped by the toxic environment at home. The financial strain can also be immense, especially if the toxic partner exerts control over resources, adding another layer of anxiety and helplessness.

The self-worth and identity of an individual are shattered. The constant criticism and belittling create a distorted self-image. One begins to believe the negative narratives spun by the toxic partner, doubting their capabilities and strengths. The dreams and aspirations that once fueled ambition are buried under layers of self-doubt and fear. The person who once had a clear sense of purpose and direction finds themselves lost, struggling to recognize the person they have become.

Yet, amidst this darkness, there is a glimmer of hope. Recognizing the profound impact of a toxic marriage on an individual is the first step towards change. It is a call to reclaim one's life, to break free from the chains that bind. The journey to healing and rediscovery is challenging, but it is also empowering. By acknowledging the effects and taking decisive action, one can begin to rebuild, to reconnect with their true self, and to forge a path towards a future filled with promise and possibility. Each step taken towards liberation is a step towards reclaiming one's power, dignity, and joy.

Impact on the Family

Imagine a household where the air feels thick, where every word can ignite a blaze, and where silence is more deafening than any argument. This is the reality of a toxic marriage—a reality that doesn't just affect the couple at its center but reverberates through the entire family. The toxic environment seeps into every corner of the home, leaving indelible marks on everyone involved, particularly the children.

Children, the silent witnesses of marital discord, often bear the heaviest burden. They absorb the tension, the anger, and the resentment, internalizing these emotions in ways that can shape their futures. Studies have shown that children raised in toxic environments are more likely to experience anxiety, depression, and behavioral issues. They struggle academically and socially, finding it difficult to form healthy relationships. The home, which should be a sanctuary, becomes a battleground, and children are the innocent casualties.

The emotional toll on children is profound. Witnessing constant conflict between parents can instill a deep sense of insecurity and fear. They may feel torn between loyalties, unsure of who to trust or confide in. This emotional turmoil can manifest in various ways—withdrawal, aggression, or even physical symptoms like headaches and stomachaches. The psychological scars can last a lifetime, affecting their self-esteem and their ability to navigate future relationships.

But it's not just the children who suffer. Extended family members, too, feel the ripple effects of a toxic marriage. Grandparents, aunts, uncles, and cousins may find themselves caught in the crossfire, often forced to take sides or mediate conflicts. These dynamics can strain familial bonds, leading to isolation and estrangement. The once tight-knit family becomes fragmented, each member grappling with the fallout in their own way.

The financial implications of a toxic marriage further compound the stress and strain on the family. Legal fees, therapy costs, and potential job losses due to emotional distress can create a precarious financial situation. Financial instability adds another layer of anxiety, making it even harder for family members to find a sense of stability and peace. The dream of a secure, happy family life feels increasingly out of reach.

Moreover, the impact on the couple themselves cannot be understated. The constant stress and emotional drain can lead to physical health problems, such as high blood pressure, heart disease, and weakened immune systems. The mental health toll is equally severe, with increased risks of depression, anxiety, and substance abuse. The individuals in the toxic marriage find themselves in a perpetual state of fight or flight, unable to truly relax or find joy.

However, breaking free from a toxic marriage isn't just an escape; it's an act of courage and a step towards healing—for everyone involved. It is an opportunity to rebuild, to create a healthier environment where each family member can thrive. Seeking help, whether through therapy, support groups, or legal counsel, can provide the necessary tools to navigate this challenging transition. The journey may be difficult, but the reward is a future where the air is lighter, the words are kinder, and the silence is filled with peace rather than dread.

The impact of a toxic marriage on the family is undeniable and far-reaching. Yet, acknowledging this impact is the first step towards change. By taking action, families can break the cycle of toxicity and pave the way for a brighter, healthier future. The chains of a toxic marriage are heavy, but they can be broken, and with each link that falls away, a new chapter begins—one filled with hope, resilience, and the promise of a better tomorrow.

Societal Perception

Imagine the whispers that follow you as you walk down the street, the sideways glances and hushed conversations that seem to follow wherever you go. Society, with all its progress and enlightenment, often clings to outdated notions about marriage and divorce. The toxic marriage you find yourself ensnared in is not just a personal battle but a societal one. The weight of societal perception can feel as stifling as the marriage itself, creating invisible chains that bind you, making the thought of breaking free seem insurmountable.

The societal ideal of marriage is often painted with broad strokes of eternal togetherness, unwavering commitment, and an almost mythical level of happiness. Deviation from this narrative invites judgment, criticism, and a questioning of one's character. The reality, however, is that not all marriages are sanctuaries of love and support. Some are battlegrounds of emotional and psychological warfare, where staying together becomes an act of survival rather than a testament to love.

It is crucial to understand that societal perceptions are not infallible truths but collective opinions shaped by culture, tradition, and sometimes ignorance. When society views divorce as a failure rather than a courageous step towards self-preservation, it perpetuates the suffering of countless individuals trapped in toxic relationships. This perception needs to be challenged and redefined.

Consider the countless stories of people who have endured years of emotional abuse, manipulation, and neglect, all under the guise of maintaining societal appearances. These individuals are often lauded for their resilience in staying together, while their silent suffering goes unnoticed. The narrative must shift from glorifying endurance to celebrating the courage to reclaim one's life and well-being.

Breaking free from a toxic marriage is not an act of selfishness; it is an act of self-respect. It is a declaration that your mental health, happiness, and future are worth fighting for. Society must learn to support and uplift those who make this brave decision rather than ostracize them. By doing so, we can create an environment where individuals feel empowered to prioritize their well-being without fear of judgment.

Education and awareness are powerful tools in reshaping societal perceptions. Sharing stories of those who have successfully escaped toxic marriages can inspire others and provide a roadmap for those still trapped. Open conversations about the realities of toxic relationships can dismantle the stigma surrounding divorce and encourage a more compassionate and understanding society.

The power to change societal perception lies within each of us. By supporting friends and loved ones who face these challenges, by refusing to perpetuate harmful stereotypes, and by advocating for a more nuanced understanding of marriage and divorce, we contribute to a more empathetic and supportive society.

Choosing to leave a toxic marriage is not an admission of defeat; it is a courageous step towards a healthier, more fulfilling life. It is time to redefine what success in marriage means and to recognize that sometimes, the bravest thing one can do is to walk away. By challenging societal perceptions and supporting those who make this difficult choice, we can help break the chains that bind so many and pave the way for a future where happiness and well-being are prioritized above all else.

Chapter 2:
The Cycle of Abuse

Patterns of Abuse

In a toxic marriage, the signs of abuse can often be subtle, insidious, and easily dismissed. Yet, recognizing these patterns is the first step towards liberation. Abuse in a marriage can take many forms, from emotional manipulation to physical violence, each one eroding the victim's sense of self-worth and autonomy. It is crucial to understand that abuse is not merely about physical harm; it encompasses a range of behaviors intended to control, demean, and isolate.

One prevalent form of abuse is emotional manipulation. This can manifest as constant criticism, belittling comments, and a relentless effort to undermine one's confidence. The abuser may use words as weapons, targeting insecurities and vulnerabilities to instill doubt and fear. By chipping away at self-esteem, the abuser creates a dependency, making the victim feel incapable of surviving without them. This emotional torment can be as damaging, if not more so, than physical violence, leaving deep psychological scars.

Isolation is another tactic commonly employed by abusers. By cutting off the victim from friends, family, and support networks, the abuser ensures that their control remains unchallenged. This isolation can be achieved through various means, such as dictating who the victim can see, monitoring communications, or creating a hostile environment that discourages social interactions. The victim, left without a support system, becomes increasingly reliant on the abuser, perpetuating the cycle of control and dependency.

Financial abuse is a less obvious but equally pernicious form of control. By controlling the finances, the abuser ensures that the victim has limited resources and options for escape. This can involve restricting access to bank accounts, forbidding the victim from working, or sabotaging their career opportunities. The financial stranglehold makes it exceedingly difficult for the victim to leave the relationship, as they may lack the means to support themselves independently.

Physical abuse, while often the most visible, is just one aspect of the broader spectrum of abusive behaviors. It can range from overt acts of violence to more covert forms, such as intimidation and threats. The abuser may use physical force to instill fear and compliance, reinforcing their dominance and control. The threat of violence, even if not always acted upon, serves as a powerful tool to keep the victim in a state of perpetual fear and submission.

Sexual abuse within a marriage is another deeply damaging form of control. It involves any non-consensual sexual act or behavior that exploits the victim's body and autonomy. This can include coercion, manipulation, or outright force. The trauma from such abuse can have long-lasting effects on the victim's mental and emotional well-being, compounding the challenges of breaking free from the toxic relationship.

Recognizing these patterns of abuse is essential for anyone trapped in a toxic marriage. It is important to understand that abuse is not always overt or violent; it can be subtle, manipulative, and deeply psychological. By identifying these behaviors, victims can begin to see the reality of their situation, challenging the narrative imposed by the abuser. Awareness is the first step towards empowerment, providing the clarity needed to seek help, support, and ultimately, escape from the chains of a toxic marriage. The journey towards freedom begins with acknowledging the patterns of abuse and understanding that no one deserves to live in fear, control, or subjugation.

Manipulation Tactics

In the labyrinth of a toxic marriage, manipulation tactics often form the invisible bars of your emotional prison. These are the subtle, yet profoundly powerful, psychological strategies employed by your partner to control, demean, and ultimately subjugate you. Recognizing these tactics is the first step toward breaking free from their insidious grip.

Gaslighting stands as one of the most pernicious tools in the manipulator's arsenal. Through consistent denial, misdirection, contradiction, and lying, your partner makes you question your reality. You find yourself doubting your memory, your perceptions, and even your sanity. When your partner insists that events you clearly remember never happened, or that your feelings are invalid or exaggerated, it's not just a disagreement; it's a calculated attempt to destabilize your sense of self. This erosion of your confidence and trust in your own judgment is designed to make you increasingly dependent on the very person undermining you.

Another common tactic is emotional blackmail. This involves your partner using your deepest fears, secrets, and insecurities against you. They may threaten to reveal personal information, abandon you, or even harm themselves if you don't comply with their demands. This creates a paralyzing fear of loss, compelling you to act against your own best interests. The emotional hostage situation leaves you feeling trapped, as each action you take is dictated by the terror of the potential consequences.

Isolation is another devastating strategy. By systematically cutting you off from friends, family, and support networks, your partner ensures that their toxic influence is the dominant force in your life. They may criticize or belittle your loved ones, create conflicts to drive wedges between you and your support system, or simply monopolize your time and attention. As your world shrinks, so does your sense of autonomy and your ability to seek help.

Financial control is yet another method of manipulation. By restricting your access to money, your partner ensures your dependence on them. They may limit your spending, monitor your purchases, or outright deny you access to financial resources. This economic stranglehold makes it incredibly difficult to leave, as the practicalities of survival become intertwined with the very person causing your suffering.

The use of guilt and obligation is also a manipulative technique often wielded with precision. Your partner may play the victim, painting themselves as the one who is wronged or misunderstood. They might remind you of all they've done for you, making you feel indebted and ungrateful. This inversion of roles creates a scenario where you are constantly striving to make amends for perceived wrongs, diverting attention from their abusive behavior.

Understanding these tactics is not just an academic exercise; it is a vital step toward reclaiming your power. Each time you identify a manipulative behavior, you weaken its hold on you. Knowledge is your shield and your sword. By recognizing these strategies, you can begin to dismantle the psychological chains that bind you, paving the way toward a life of freedom and self-respect. Your awareness and resilience are your greatest allies in escaping the toxic grip of manipulation and moving toward a healthier, more fulfilling future.

Emotional Rollercoaster

The heart-wrenching turmoil that accompanies a toxic marriage can leave you feeling like you're on an emotional rollercoaster, with no end in sight. This relentless cycle of highs and lows can sap your energy, crush your spirit, and make you question your own worth. But it's crucial to recognize that this emotional upheaval is not a reflection of your own failings; rather, it is a symptom of a deeply unhealthy relationship dynamic.

Imagine waking up each day, not knowing whether you'll be met with affection or hostility. The unpredictability keeps you on edge, constantly bracing for the next emotional blow. This inconsistency is not just stressful; it's toxic. It undermines your sense of stability and security, leaving you feeling anxious and disoriented. The emotional whiplash can be so severe that you start to doubt your own perceptions and feelings, a phenomenon known as gaslighting. This manipulation is designed to keep you off balance, making it easier for your partner to exert control.

The moments of tenderness and love, though fleeting, are what keep you tethered to the relationship. These rare glimpses of affection are like breadcrumbs, leading you to believe that things might improve, that the person you fell in love with is still there, hidden beneath the layers of toxicity. But these moments are not signs of genuine change; they are part of the manipulative cycle that keeps you ensnared. They create a false sense of hope that things will get better, when in reality, they rarely do.

It's important to understand that this emotional volatility is not your fault. You are not responsible for the unpredictable behavior of your partner. Their actions are a reflection of their own issues, not of your worth or value. Recognizing this can be liberating. It allows you to see the situation for what it truly is—a toxic environment that is damaging to your emotional and mental well-being.

Taking steps to extricate yourself from this emotional chaos is an act of self-preservation. It is not easy, and it requires immense courage and strength. But the alternative is to remain trapped in a cycle that erodes your self-esteem and drains your emotional reserves. By prioritizing your own well-being, you are taking the first crucial step towards reclaiming your life and your sense of self.

Support from friends, family, and professionals can be invaluable during this time. They can provide the stability and validation that is so often lacking in a toxic relationship. Don't hesitate to reach out for help; you don't have to go through this alone. Surrounding yourself with a network of supportive individuals can make a world of difference as you navigate this challenging terrain.

Breaking free from the emotional rollercoaster of a toxic marriage is not just about ending a relationship; it's about reclaiming your life. It's about recognizing your own worth and refusing to settle for anything less than you deserve. It's about finding the strength to say enough is enough, and taking the bold steps necessary to build a healthier, happier future. You have the power to change your story, to step off the rollercoaster, and to start living a life free from the chains of emotional turmoil.

The Honeymoon Phase

Imagine a time when everything seemed perfect. Love was new, passion was intense, and every moment spent together felt like a dream. This was the honeymoon phase, a period that can be as misleading as it is magical. The euphoria of this stage often masks deeper, more troubling issues that might be lurking beneath the surface. Understanding this phase is crucial for anyone seeking to escape the chains of a toxic marriage.

In the honeymoon phase, your partner may go to great lengths to win your affection. Grand gestures, thoughtful surprises, and constant attention create an illusion of perfection. You feel valued, adored, and even cherished. But it's important to recognize that this intense focus on you might not be sustainable. It's not uncommon for toxic individuals to use this phase to establish control and dependency. They reel you in with kindness and generosity, setting the stage for later manipulation.

During this period, you might find yourself overlooking red flags. Minor disagreements are easily dismissed, and any odd behavior is often rationalized away. "It's just a rough patch," you tell yourself, or "Everyone has flaws." These justifications create a dangerous precedent. The longer you ignore these warning signs, the more entrenched you become in a relationship that could ultimately be harmful.

The illusion of the honeymoon phase can make it difficult to see the true nature of your partner. They might seem perfect, but perfection is a mask that can hide deeper, more troubling traits. For instance, excessive jealousy might be disguised as caring. Controlling behavior might be framed as protectiveness. These traits, if left unchecked, can evolve into more toxic patterns of behavior.

Acknowledging the temporary nature of this phase is essential. No relationship can sustain the intense passion and idealization indefinitely. As the initial excitement wanes, the true dynamics of the relationship begin to emerge. This transition can be jarring, especially if you've been swept up in the fairy tale. The shift can reveal a partner who is not as kind, considerate, or loving as they initially appeared.

It's also important to consider the impact of this phase on your own behavior. The desire to maintain the honeymoon illusion can lead you to compromise your values and needs. You might find yourself constantly trying to please your partner, sacrificing your own happiness in the process. This self-neglect can erode your sense of self-worth, making it even harder to recognize and address the toxic dynamics at play.

To break free from a toxic marriage, it's crucial to see through the facade of the honeymoon phase. Reflect on the early days of your relationship with a critical eye. Were there signs of control, jealousy, or manipulation that you ignored? Did you feel pressured to conform to your partner's expectations? Identifying these patterns can provide valuable insights into the true nature of your relationship.

Don't let the memory of the honeymoon phase keep you chained to a toxic partner. The initial magic might have been real, but it was also fleeting. True love is built on mutual respect, trust, and genuine care, not on a foundation of manipulation and control. Recognize the honeymoon phase for what it is—a temporary stage—and use this understanding to empower yourself. Your journey to freedom begins with seeing through the illusion and reclaiming your strength.

Breaking the Cycle

In the harrowing maze of a toxic marriage, it can feel as though the walls are closing in, and the path to freedom is obscured by doubt and fear. Yet, there exists a powerful truth: you have the strength to break free from these suffocating chains. The first step is recognizing that the cycle of toxicity is not an unchangeable fate but a pattern that can be disrupted and redefined.

Imagine for a moment the life you yearn for, a life where respect, love, and mutual understanding are the cornerstones of your relationship. This vision is not a mere fantasy; it is an attainable reality. The key lies in identifying and dismantling the destructive patterns that have taken root in your marriage. Toxic cycles often thrive on unspoken resentments, unchecked anger, and a lack of communication. By addressing these elements head-on, you can begin to erode the foundation of toxicity.

Communication is the lifeblood of any healthy relationship. It is the bridge that connects two souls, allowing them to share their deepest fears, desires, and aspirations. In a toxic marriage, this bridge is often in disrepair, marred by misunderstandings and emotional wounds. To mend it, both partners must be willing to engage in open, honest dialogue. This means expressing feelings without fear of retribution and listening without judgment. It is a daunting task, but one that is essential for healing.

Equally important is the need to establish boundaries. In a toxic relationship, boundaries are frequently blurred or outright ignored, leading to a sense of entrapment and helplessness. Clear, firm boundaries serve as a protective barrier, safeguarding your emotional and mental well-being. They define what is acceptable and what is not, giving you the power to say no to harmful behaviors and yes to self-respect and dignity.

Self-reflection is another critical tool in breaking the cycle of toxicity. It requires a willingness to look inward, to examine your own behaviors and attitudes that may be contributing to the unhealthy dynamics. This is not about assigning blame but about understanding and growth. By acknowledging your role in the cycle, you empower yourself to make conscious, positive changes.

Support systems play a vital role in this transformative process. Surround yourself with friends, family, or support groups who can offer encouragement, perspective, and practical advice. Isolation is a breeding ground for toxicity, whereas connection fosters resilience and hope.

It is also essential to recognize that breaking free from a toxic marriage may require professional help. Therapists and counselors are trained to navigate the complexities of relationship dynamics and can provide invaluable guidance and strategies for change. Seeking help is not a sign of weakness but a testament to your commitment to a healthier, happier life.

The journey to breaking the cycle of toxicity is undoubtedly challenging, but the rewards are profound. Imagine a life where you wake up each day feeling valued and cherished, where your interactions are marked by kindness and respect. This is not an impossible dream but a potential reality waiting to be realized. The power to change your life is within you, and by taking deliberate, courageous steps, you can escape the chains of a toxic marriage and create a future filled with hope and possibility.

Chapter 3:
The Psychology of Toxic Relationships

The Abuser's Mindset

Understanding the dynamics of a toxic marriage requires delving into the mindset of the abuser. It is essential to comprehend that abusers often operate under a calculated pattern of manipulation, control, and domination. These individuals are not driven by love, but by a need to exert power over their partners, often stemming from deep-seated insecurities and unresolved personal traumas.

The abuser's mindset is rooted in a distorted perception of relationships. They view their partner not as an equal, but as a possession to be controlled. This mentality fuels their actions and justifies their behavior in their own eyes. They believe that by maintaining control, they can prevent their partner from leaving or challenging their authority. This need for control manifests in various forms, from emotional manipulation to physical violence.

Abusers often employ tactics of isolation, keeping their partner away from friends and family to weaken their support system. By doing so, they make their partner more dependent on them, fostering a sense of helplessness and entrapment. This isolation is a strategic move to ensure that the victim feels they have no one else to turn to, making it easier for the abuser to maintain dominance.

Furthermore, abusers are adept at gaslighting, a psychological manipulation technique that makes the victim question their own reality and sanity. By constantly denying the truth, twisting facts, and shifting blame, the abuser creates a confusing and disorienting environment. This tactic is designed to destabilize the victim's sense of self and make them more compliant.

The abuser's need for control is often masked by a façade of charm and charisma, especially in the early stages of the relationship. They may shower their partner with affection, gifts, and attention, creating a whirlwind romance that can be intoxicating. However, this charm is a tool to gain trust and establish a bond, which is later exploited to manipulate and control the victim.

It is also important to recognize that abusers often have a skewed sense of entitlement. They believe they are justified in their actions and that their partner owes them obedience and loyalty. This sense of entitlement can lead to explosive reactions when the abuser feels their control is being threatened. Any act of independence or defiance by the victim is met with punishment, reinforcing the abuser's dominance.

Moreover, abusers frequently employ a cycle of abuse that includes periods of tension building, explosive incidents of abuse, and phases of reconciliation. During the reconciliation phase, the abuser may apologize, make promises to change, and temporarily revert to their charming behavior. This cycle creates a confusing and emotionally turbulent environment for the victim, making it difficult for them to break free.

Understanding the abuser's mindset is crucial for recognizing the signs of a toxic marriage and taking steps to escape it. Abusers thrive on power and control, and their manipulative tactics are deeply ingrained. Recognizing these patterns is the first step towards breaking free from the chains of a toxic relationship and reclaiming one's sense of self and independence. Empowerment begins with awareness, and by understanding the abuser's mindset, one can begin to dismantle the control they hold and move towards a healthier, happier future.

The Victim's Perspective

Imagine waking up each day with a knot of dread tightening in your stomach, knowing that the person who promised to love and cherish you is the very source of your anguish. This is the harsh reality for countless individuals trapped in toxic marriages. The scars inflicted by such unions are not just physical but emotional, leaving deep, invisible wounds that fester over time. These victims often find themselves ensnared in a web of manipulation, control, and fear, struggling to reclaim their sense of self-worth and autonomy.

Toxic marriages thrive on power imbalances. The abuser wields control through a myriad of tactics—belittlement, isolation, and gaslighting are just a few. The victim, often painted as the problem, internalizes this narrative, leading to a debilitating sense of guilt and self-blame. It's a vicious cycle: the more the victims try to appease their partners, the more the abusers tighten their grip, perpetuating a relentless cycle of emotional abuse.

Financial dependence is another chain that binds victims to their toxic partners. Many abusers ensure that their spouses remain economically reliant, stripping them of the means to escape. This financial stranglehold is a powerful weapon, leaving the victim feeling trapped and powerless. The fear of starting over with nothing, coupled with the abuser's threats of financial ruin, can paralyze even the strongest of spirits.

The impact on mental health cannot be overstated. Anxiety, depression, and post-traumatic stress disorder (PTSD) are common afflictions among those in toxic marriages. The constant state of hypervigilance—always walking on eggshells, anticipating the next outburst—takes a severe toll on the psyche. Over time, the victims' sense of reality becomes so distorted that they begin to doubt their own perceptions, making it even harder to recognize the need for escape.

Children, too, are silent sufferers in these toxic environments. They absorb the tension, the fear, and the dysfunction, which can manifest in myriad ways—behavioral issues, academic struggles, and emotional disturbances. Witnessing a parent being demeaned and controlled teaches them harmful lessons about relationships and self-worth. The cycle of abuse can perpetuate across generations if not broken.

Yet, the societal stigma surrounding divorce and the myth of the 'perfect family' often compels victims to stay silent. They fear judgment, ostracization, and the label of 'failure.' This societal pressure, coupled with the abuser's manipulative tactics, creates an almost insurmountable barrier to seeking help. Friends and family, often unaware of the extent of the abuse, may inadvertently reinforce the victims' isolation by urging them to 'make it work' or 'stay for the children.'

The narrative must shift from one of silent suffering to one of empowerment and support. Recognizing the signs of a toxic marriage is the first crucial step. Education and awareness can dismantle the myths surrounding these relationships, offering victims a lifeline of understanding and compassion. Communities must rally around those in distress, providing resources, safe havens, and emotional support.

Escape is not just a physical act but a profound psychological journey towards reclaiming one's life and identity. Every individual deserves to live free from fear and oppression. By listening, believing, and offering unwavering support, we can help victims of toxic marriages break their chains and step into a future filled with hope and healing.

Trauma Bonding

Imagine waking up each day feeling trapped in an emotional prison, where the very person who should offer love and support inflicts pain and confusion instead. This is the cruel reality of trauma bonding, a phenomenon that keeps countless individuals shackled to toxic marriages. It's a bond so powerful, it can feel unbreakable, yet understanding its nature is the first crucial step in reclaiming one's freedom.

Trauma bonding occurs when a cycle of abuse and intermittent reinforcement creates a powerful emotional attachment. It's a sinister dance of highs and lows, where moments of affection and kindness are interspersed with periods of cruelty and neglect. These fleeting moments of love become like breadcrumbs, leading you deeper into the labyrinth of emotional dependency. The abuser's manipulative tactics exploit your vulnerabilities, making you question your worth and reality.

One of the most insidious aspects of trauma bonding is its ability to warp your perception. You begin to rationalize the abuser's behavior, convincing yourself that the good times outweigh the bad, or that you somehow deserve the mistreatment. This cognitive dissonance keeps you ensnared, as you cling to the hope that things will improve or that you can change the abuser's behavior through your actions.

The impact of trauma bonding extends beyond emotional turmoil; it affects every facet of your life. Your self-esteem erodes, and you may find yourself isolated from friends and family who could offer support. The abuser often employs tactics like gaslighting, making you doubt your own memories and perceptions. This psychological warfare leaves you feeling disoriented and dependent on the abuser for a sense of reality.

Breaking free from trauma bonding requires a profound shift in perspective. Recognizing that the abuser's intermittent kindness is a calculated tactic to maintain control is a vital revelation. It's essential to understand that you are not at fault for the abuse, nor is it within your power to change the abuser's behavior. This awareness can be both liberating and terrifying, as it shatters the illusion of control and exposes the depth of manipulation you've endured.

Support systems play a crucial role in dismantling the chains of trauma bonding. Reaching out to trusted friends, family, or professionals can provide the validation and encouragement needed to take the first steps toward freedom. Therapy can be particularly beneficial, offering a safe space to explore your experiences and rebuild your sense of self-worth. Cognitive-behavioral techniques can help reframe negative thought patterns and develop healthier coping mechanisms.

Empowerment comes from reclaiming your narrative and asserting your right to a life free from abuse. Setting boundaries and prioritizing self-care are acts of defiance against the abuser's control. It's a journey that requires immense courage and resilience, but each step forward is a testament to your strength and capacity for healing.

In the end, breaking the bonds of trauma is not just about escaping a toxic marriage; it's about rediscovering your autonomy and embracing a future where your worth is no longer defined by another's cruelty. It's about forging a path to a life where love is not a weapon, but a source of genuine support and joy.

Cognitive Dissonance

Imagine waking up every day to a life that feels like a never-ending storm, where the person who once promised to love and cherish you is now the source of your deepest wounds. You tell yourself it's not that bad, that you can endure it, that things will get better. Yet, deep down, you know something is terribly wrong. This internal conflict, this emotional tug-of-war, is the essence of cognitive dissonance—a psychological phenomenon that can keep you shackled in a toxic marriage far longer than you ever intended.

Cognitive dissonance occurs when you hold two contradictory beliefs or attitudes simultaneously. For example, you may believe that you deserve happiness and respect, yet you stay in a relationship where you are neither happy nor respected. This dissonance creates an unsettling tension that your mind desperately wants to resolve. The easiest way to do this is often to rationalize the situation, to convince yourself that the abuse isn't as bad as it seems, or that your partner will change. But these rationalizations are nothing more than illusions, designed to keep you in a state of paralysis.

The mind is a powerful tool, capable of extraordinary feats of self-deception. It can create a narrative where you are the hero enduring great trials for the sake of love or family. This narrative can be so compelling that it blinds you to the reality of your suffering. You might tell yourself that leaving would mean giving up, that it would make you a failure. But these thoughts are not truths; they are the chains that bind you to your misery.

Recognizing cognitive dissonance is the first step toward liberation. It requires a brutal honesty with yourself, a willingness to confront the painful truths you've been avoiding. Ask yourself: Why do I feel the need to justify my partner's behavior? Why do I downplay my own pain? These questions can illuminate the dissonance at play, revealing the mental gymnastics you've been performing to maintain a semblance of normalcy.

Once you acknowledge the dissonance, the next step is to dismantle it. This involves challenging the beliefs that keep you stuck. Start by affirming your right to a life free from emotional and physical harm. Remind yourself that love should not hurt, that a healthy relationship is built on mutual respect and support. Surround yourself with voices of reason—friends, family, or a therapist—who can offer a perspective unclouded by the fog of your dissonance.

Taking action is crucial. Small steps can lead to monumental change. Begin by setting boundaries, even if they're just mental ones at first. Recognize that you have the power to change your situation, that you are not powerless. Each boundary you set, each step you take toward independence, weakens the hold of cognitive dissonance.

The journey out of a toxic marriage is fraught with challenges, but understanding cognitive dissonance can be your guiding light. It helps you see the chains for what they are—illusions created by a mind struggling to reconcile the irreconcilable. By confronting these illusions, you can begin to break free, reclaiming the life and happiness you deserve.

The Power of Manipulation

In the labyrinth of a toxic marriage, manipulation is a weapon wielded with precision and subtlety. It's an insidious force that seeps into the crevices of your relationship, eroding trust and autonomy. Recognizing its presence is the first step toward reclaiming your power and sanity. Manipulation often masquerades as care, concern, or even love, making it difficult to identify. But once you peel back the layers, the truth becomes glaringly obvious: it's about control.

Picture this: your partner showers you with affection and gifts, but only when you've acted according to their wishes. This isn't generosity; it's a transaction. The underlying message is clear: your worth is conditional. Such tactics are designed to keep you tethered, to make you question your own judgment and reality. Over time, you might find yourself walking on eggshells, constantly seeking approval, and doubting your every move.

Gaslighting is another potent tool in the manipulator's arsenal. This psychological tactic involves making you question your memory, perception, and sanity. Imagine recalling an event with clarity, only for your partner to insist it never happened or that you're exaggerating. This relentless assault on your reality can leave you disoriented and dependent, eroding your confidence and self-worth.

Isolation is equally devastating. By subtly or overtly discouraging your relationships with friends and family, manipulators ensure that their influence is unchallenged. They might criticize your loved ones, create conflicts, or simply monopolize your time. The goal is to make you increasingly reliant on them for emotional support, validation, and social interaction. When you're cut off from your support network, their control over you strengthens.

Emotional blackmail is another weapon of choice. Phrases like, "If you really loved me, you would..." or "Look what you made me do," are designed to guilt-trip you into compliance. This manipulative strategy twists your emotions, making you feel responsible for their happiness and actions. It's a pernicious way to keep you in a state of perpetual guilt and obligation.

Financial control is yet another dimension of manipulation. By controlling the purse strings, your partner ensures that you remain financially dependent. They might scrutinize your spending, withhold money, or sabotage your job prospects. This economic stranglehold makes it incredibly difficult to leave, as the fear of financial instability looms large.

The cumulative effect of these manipulative tactics is devastating. They strip you of your autonomy, erode your self-esteem, and distort your perception of reality. But knowledge is power. By recognizing these behaviors for what they are, you can begin to dismantle their hold over you. Trust your instincts and validate your experiences. Seek support from trusted friends, family, or professional counselors who can offer an outside perspective and bolster your resolve.

Manipulation thrives in the shadows, but once exposed to the light of awareness, its power diminishes. You deserve a relationship built on mutual respect, trust, and genuine love. By confronting and addressing manipulation, you take the first courageous step toward breaking free from the chains of a toxic marriage. Your journey to reclaiming your life and autonomy starts with recognizing the manipulative tactics at play and refusing to let them define your reality.

Chapter 4:
Acknowledge, Accept, Act

Realizing the Reality

Imagine waking up every day with a sense of dread, feeling the weight of a relationship that no longer brings joy or fulfillment. Many individuals find themselves trapped in toxic marriages, where love has been replaced by resentment, fear, and emotional turmoil. It's easy to ignore the signs, to convince oneself that things will get better, or to believe that enduring the pain is a necessary sacrifice. But the first step to freedom is acknowledging the truth of the situation.

The illusion of a perfect marriage is often perpetuated by societal expectations and personal fears. We are taught to believe that enduring hardship is a testament to our strength and commitment. However, there is a stark difference between facing challenges together and being subjected to constant emotional abuse and neglect. Recognizing this distinction is crucial. A toxic marriage erodes self-esteem, stifles personal growth, and can even have severe impacts on mental and physical health.

Denial is a powerful force. It whispers that things aren't really that bad, that perhaps it's all in your head, or that you are the one to blame. Yet, deep down, the signs are clear. Frequent arguments, feelings of worthlessness, and a pervasive sense of unhappiness are not the hallmarks of a healthy relationship. It's important to confront these feelings head-on, to peel back the layers of denial and see the reality for what it is.

You deserve to live a life filled with love, respect, and happiness. The fear of the unknown can be paralyzing, but staying in a toxic marriage is a guarantee of continued suffering. Many people stay because they fear judgment, worry about financial instability, or dread the impact on children. These concerns are valid, but they should not be the chains that bind you to a life of misery.

Consider the long-term effects of remaining in such an environment. The constant stress and emotional strain can lead to anxiety, depression, and a host of other health issues. Children who grow up in toxic households often carry the scars into their adult lives, affecting their relationships and self-worth. By choosing to stay, you are not protecting anyone—you are perpetuating a cycle of pain.

It's time to shift the narrative. Leaving a toxic marriage is not a failure; it is an act of courage and self-preservation. It's a declaration that you value yourself and your well-being enough to seek a better life. Surround yourself with supportive friends and family, seek professional help if needed, and start planning a path to freedom. The road may be challenging, but the destination is worth every step.

Visualize a future where you wake up feeling hopeful and at peace. Imagine building a life that reflects your true desires and aspirations. This is not just a dream—it is a possibility within your reach. The first and most crucial step is to recognize the reality of your situation. Take a deep breath, look in the mirror, and acknowledge the truth. It's time to break free from the chains of a toxic marriage and reclaim your life.

Accepting Your Situation

In the turmoil of a toxic marriage, the most challenging yet crucial step is to acknowledge the reality of your situation. It requires immense courage to face the truth, but this acceptance is the foundation upon which you can build a path to freedom. Denial may seem like a protective shield, but it only prolongs the inevitable and deepens the wounds. Confronting the harsh reality head-on is the first act of reclaiming your life.

Living in a toxic marriage often means enduring a daily barrage of emotional manipulation, psychological abuse, and perhaps even physical harm. You may find yourself constantly second-guessing your worth, questioning your sanity, and losing sight of who you truly are. It's essential to understand that this is not your fault. The blame lies squarely on the shoulders of the one who perpetuates this toxic environment. Accepting this truth is not about assigning blame, but about recognizing the situation for what it is—a necessary step towards liberation.

Your mind might be clouded with doubt, fear, and guilt. You might be telling yourself that things will get better, that your partner will change, or that you can somehow fix the situation. However, these thoughts only serve to keep you trapped in a cycle of pain. Acknowledging that your marriage is toxic is not a sign of failure; it's a testament to your strength and clarity. It is an awakening to the fact that you deserve better—a life filled with respect, love, and genuine happiness.

One common obstacle in this process is the fear of the unknown. The idea of leaving a toxic marriage can be terrifying, especially when you've been conditioned to believe that you are incapable of surviving on your own. But remember, the unknown holds endless possibilities for growth and healing. The first step towards these possibilities is accepting where you are now. This acceptance is not about resigning to your fate but about understanding your present circumstances so you can take informed, deliberate actions towards change.

Support systems play a pivotal role in this phase. Reach out to trusted friends, family members, or professional counselors who can offer a different perspective and provide the emotional support you need. Sometimes, an external viewpoint can illuminate the reality of your situation in ways you hadn't considered. These individuals can help you validate your feelings and experiences, reinforcing the importance of your well-being.

Accepting your situation also involves practical considerations. Take stock of your resources, both emotional and financial. Knowing what you have at your disposal can empower you to make practical plans for your future. It is about equipping yourself with the knowledge and tools necessary to break free from the chains that bind you.

Every small step you take in acknowledging your reality is a step towards reclaiming your power. It's about shifting your mindset from one of helplessness to one of empowerment. By accepting your situation, you are not giving up hope; you are igniting a spark of resilience and determination. This acceptance is the catalyst for change, the moment when you decide that enough is enough, and you deserve a life free from toxic chains.

So, stand tall and face the truth. It is the bravest thing you can do. Accept your situation, not as a defeat, but as the first victory in your journey towards a brighter, healthier, and happier future.

Choosing to Act

Taking control of your life and making the decision to act can be the most liberating choice you ever make. Toxic marriages have a way of chaining you down, making you feel powerless and defeated. But it's crucial to understand that you hold the key to your freedom. The first step is recognizing that you have the power to change your circumstances. This realization can be transformative, altering the way you see yourself and your situation.

Imagine living a life where your happiness and well-being are at the forefront. Picture a world where you are no longer subjected to constant emotional turmoil. This isn't just a distant fantasy; it's a real possibility. The act of deciding to leave a toxic marriage is not an act of cowardice or failure, but one of immense bravery. It takes courage to confront the reality of your situation and to acknowledge that you deserve better.

Fear is a natural response when facing the unknown, but it should not paralyze you. Fear can be a powerful motivator, pushing you to take steps you never thought possible. Use it to your advantage. Channel your fear into action, and let it fuel your determination to reclaim your life. Every small step you take towards leaving your toxic marriage is a victory. Each action, no matter how minor it may seem, brings you closer to a life of peace and joy.

Support systems play a crucial role in this process. Surround yourself with people who genuinely care about your well-being. Friends, family, and support groups can provide the encouragement and strength you need. They can offer a different perspective, helping you see possibilities you might have overlooked. Lean on them, and don't hesitate to ask for help. You are not alone in this journey; countless others have walked this path and emerged stronger.

Financial independence is another critical aspect to consider. Toxic marriages often involve financial control, making it difficult to envision a life apart. Start by taking small steps towards financial autonomy. Open a separate bank account, if you haven't already. Create a budget that allows you to save money discreetly. Seek professional advice if necessary. Financial independence can significantly ease the transition and provide a sense of security.

It's also essential to prioritize your mental and emotional health. Toxic marriages can leave deep scars, affecting your self-esteem and overall mental well-being. Consider seeking therapy or counseling to help you process your emotions and develop coping strategies. Self-care should not be an afterthought; it's a necessity. Engage in activities that bring you joy and help you relax. Whether it's reading, exercising, or spending time with loved ones, make time for yourself.

Taking action means different things for different people. For some, it may mean seeking legal advice and starting the divorce process. For others, it might involve creating a safety plan and finding a secure place to stay. Whatever your path, the important thing is to keep moving forward. Stagnation only prolongs the suffering and keeps you chained to a life of misery.

You have the strength within you to break free from the chains of a toxic marriage. You deserve a life filled with love, respect, and happiness. The decision to act is the first and most crucial step towards that life. Take it, and never look back.

Facing the Fear

Fear is often the most formidable barrier preventing individuals from breaking free from a toxic marriage. It paralyzes, distorts reality, and makes the unknown seem insurmountable. Yet, it is essential to recognize that fear is not an insurmountable obstacle; it is a challenge that can be confronted and overcome. The first step towards liberation is acknowledging that fear exists and understanding its root causes.

Imagine living in a constant state of dread, where every action is scrutinized, and every word is a potential trigger for conflict. This is the reality of a toxic marriage. However, the fear of leaving this environment can be even more overwhelming. The fear of the unknown, financial instability, societal judgment, and the emotional toll on children are all valid concerns. But these fears should not be the chains that bind you to a life of misery.

Consider the alternative: a life where you reclaim your self-worth, rediscover your passions, and rebuild your confidence. This vision is not a distant dream but a reachable reality. The fear of leaving is often rooted in the fear of failure. Yet, staying in a toxic marriage is a failure to yourself and your potential. You owe it to yourself to seek happiness and fulfillment, and this journey begins by facing your fears head-on.

One powerful way to confront fear is through education and preparation. Knowledge is empowering. Understanding your legal rights, financial options, and available support systems can alleviate much of the anxiety associated with leaving a toxic marriage. Reach out to professionals, such as attorneys, financial advisors, and therapists, who can provide you with the information and support you need. Equip yourself with the tools and resources necessary to make informed decisions about your future.

Support networks play a crucial role in overcoming fear. Friends, family, and support groups can offer emotional backing and practical assistance. Surround yourself with individuals who uplift and encourage you. Their strength can bolster your resolve, and their experiences can provide valuable insights. You are not alone in this struggle; many have faced similar fears and emerged stronger and happier. Their stories are testaments to the fact that fear can be conquered.

Visualize the life you desire. Picture yourself free from the toxic environment that currently engulfs you. Envision a home filled with peace, joy, and mutual respect. This mental image can serve as a powerful motivator. It is a reminder of what you are striving for and why it is worth facing your fears. This vision can fuel your determination and give you the courage to take the necessary steps towards achieving it.

Taking action is the ultimate antidote to fear. Small, incremental steps can lead to significant changes. Start by setting achievable goals. Whether it's saving money, seeking legal advice, or having an honest conversation with a trusted friend, each step brings you closer to your goal. Celebrate these small victories as they build momentum and reinforce your confidence.

Fear will always be a part of the human experience, but it does not have to dictate your life choices. By confronting and managing your fears, you can break free from the chains of a toxic marriage and create a future filled with hope and possibility. It is within your power to transform fear into a catalyst for change. The life you deserve is on the other side of fear; take the first step towards it today.

Taking the First Step

Imagine a life where every breath you take is free from the suffocating grip of a toxic marriage. This isn't just a distant dream; it's a reality within your reach. The first step toward liberation is often the hardest, but it is also the most crucial. Your future, your happiness, and your well-being depend on this pivotal moment.

The chains that bind you in a toxic relationship are not unbreakable. They may seem formidable, but they are not insurmountable. You have the strength within you to shatter them, one link at a time. The initial stride toward freedom is acknowledging that you deserve better. You deserve respect, love, and a life unmarred by constant negativity and emotional turmoil.

Taking that first step requires courage, but courage is not the absence of fear; it is the determination to move forward despite it. Recognize that fear is a natural response to change, especially when that change involves leaving behind something familiar, even if it is harmful. However, staying in a toxic environment only perpetuates the cycle of pain and diminishes your spirit.

Consider the impact of remaining in a toxic marriage not just on yourself, but on those around you. If there are children involved, think about the lessons they are learning from your relationship. They deserve to see a model of healthy, respectful love. By taking the first step, you are not only freeing yourself but also setting a powerful example for them.

The journey to breaking free begins with a single, decisive action. This could be seeking support from friends or family, consulting a therapist, or reaching out to a support group. Surround yourself with people who believe in you and your right to a better life. Their encouragement will be an invaluable source of strength as you navigate this challenging path.

Another crucial aspect is educating yourself about the dynamics of toxic relationships. Understanding the patterns and behaviors that characterize such marriages can provide clarity and reinforce your resolve. Knowledge is power, and it will arm you with the tools needed to dismantle the toxic structures that have held you captive.

Financial independence is another significant consideration. Evaluate your financial situation and take steps to secure your economic stability. This might involve seeking employment, enhancing your skills, or consulting a financial advisor. Financial security will provide you with the confidence and means to stand on your own.

As you prepare to take this monumental step, remember to be kind to yourself. Self-compassion is essential. Acknowledge the bravery it takes to make this decision and allow yourself to feel proud of the progress you are making. Healing is a process, and every step forward, no matter how small, is a victory.

Visualize the life you want to create for yourself, a life filled with peace, joy, and genuine love. Let this vision be your guiding star, illuminating the path ahead. You have the power to transform your reality, to break free from the chains that have bound you, and to step into a future where you are empowered and cherished.

This is your moment. Take that first step. Your new life is waiting.

Chapter 5:
Planning Your Escape

Creating a Safety Plan

In the midst of a toxic marriage, the importance of a well-structured safety plan cannot be overstated. It represents the first crucial step in reclaiming control of your life and ensuring your well-being. A safety plan is not just a set of guidelines; it is a lifeline that can make the difference between enduring ongoing harm and securing a brighter, healthier future for yourself.

Imagine the peace of mind that comes from knowing you have a clear, actionable strategy in place. This plan is your personal blueprint for navigating the complexities and dangers that often accompany leaving a toxic relationship. It empowers you to take decisive action, anticipate challenges, and protect yourself from further harm.

The first element of a robust safety plan is securing a safe place to go. Whether it's a trusted friend's house, a family member's home, or a dedicated shelter, knowing you have a refuge is paramount. This location should be somewhere your partner cannot easily access, ensuring that you can find immediate and sustained safety.

Next, consider the importance of financial independence. Toxic relationships often come with financial control and manipulation. Begin by setting aside small amounts of money in a separate account, if possible. Even a modest sum can provide the means to escape and sustain yourself in the initial stages. Additionally, gather important documents—identification, financial records, legal papers—and store them in a secure, accessible location. These documents are essential for establishing your new life and protecting your legal rights.

Communication is another critical aspect. Identify a few trusted individuals who can offer support and keep them informed about your situation. Develop a code word or phrase that signals you need immediate help. This discreet form of communication can be a lifeline in moments of urgent need.

Technology can also be an ally in your safety plan. Ensure your digital communications are secure by changing passwords and using encrypted messaging services. Be mindful of your online presence and the information you share, as abusers often monitor these channels to exert control.

Moreover, understand the legal protections available to you. Familiarize yourself with local laws and resources, such as restraining orders and domestic violence hotlines. Legal measures can provide an additional layer of security and peace of mind, reinforcing your safety plan.

Mental and emotional preparation is equally important. Leaving a toxic marriage is an emotional rollercoaster, and building a support network of friends, family, or professional counselors can provide the strength and encouragement needed to persevere. These individuals can offer a listening ear, practical advice, and emotional support, helping you navigate the complexities of your situation.

Finally, rehearse your plan. Practice how you will leave, what you will take, and where you will go. This rehearsal can help reduce panic and confusion during the actual departure, making the process smoother and more manageable.

A safety plan is your proactive stance against the chaos of a toxic marriage. It equips you with the tools and strategies necessary to protect yourself and build a future free from abuse. By taking these steps, you are not just planning an escape; you are laying the foundation for a life of dignity, security, and hope.

Building a Support Network

Imagine standing at the edge of a daunting cliff, looking down at the tumultuous waters below, knowing you must leap but feeling paralyzed by fear. This is what it often feels like to consider leaving a toxic marriage. The isolation, the self-doubt, the manipulation—these chains weigh heavily on your spirit. Yet, there is a lifeline, a beacon of hope that can guide you through the dark and stormy seas: building a support network.

The significance of a robust support network cannot be overstated. It serves as both a safety net and a springboard, catching you when you fall and propelling you toward a brighter future. Surrounding yourself with people who genuinely care for your well-being can make an insurmountable task seem achievable. These individuals will not only offer practical help but also emotional sustenance, which is often equally, if not more, vital.

One of the first steps in constructing this network is identifying who can be part of it. Friends and family are obvious choices, but it's crucial to select those who understand the gravity of your situation and can provide unwavering support. Not everyone will be able to comprehend the complexities of a toxic relationship, and that's okay. Focus on those who listen without judgment, who offer encouragement rather than criticism, and who respect your decisions even if they don't fully grasp your experiences.

Professional help is another cornerstone of a solid support network. Therapists, counselors, and support groups provide specialized guidance that friends and family may not be equipped to offer. These professionals can help you navigate the emotional labyrinth that often accompanies the end of a toxic marriage. They provide a safe space to explore your feelings, develop coping strategies, and build resilience. Moreover, their expertise can be invaluable in helping you reclaim your sense of self-worth and autonomy, which are often eroded in such relationships.

Don't underestimate the power of community organizations and online forums. These platforms can offer a sense of belonging and validation that is incredibly empowering. Many people have walked the same path and have emerged stronger on the other side. Their stories can serve as both inspiration and practical advice. Engaging with these communities can help you feel less alone and more understood, which is a crucial element in the healing process.

It's essential to be proactive in nurturing these relationships. Regularly communicate with your support network, updating them on your progress and setbacks. This not only keeps them informed but also reinforces the bond you share. Remember, this network is a two-way street; while they provide support, your openness and willingness to engage are equally important.

In moments of doubt and despair, your support network can be the anchor that keeps you grounded. They remind you of your strength, your worth, and your potential for a happier future. They help you see through the fog of fear and uncertainty, illuminating the path to freedom and self-discovery.

Taking the step to leave a toxic marriage is undoubtedly one of the most challenging decisions you will ever make. However, with a strong support network, you are not alone. You have a team of allies who believe in you, who will stand by you, and who will help you navigate the rocky terrain ahead. This collective strength can transform what seems like an insurmountable challenge into a journey of empowerment and liberation.

Financial Independence

Imagine a life where you are no longer shackled by the financial constraints imposed by a toxic marriage. Picture waking up each day knowing that you have the freedom to make decisions for yourself and your children, without the looming fear of financial instability. This vision is not a distant dream; it is a tangible reality that can be achieved through financial independence.

Financial independence is the cornerstone of breaking free from a toxic relationship. It empowers you to take control of your life, offering a sense of security and stability that is crucial during and after the tumultuous period of leaving a toxic partner. The first step towards this independence is understanding your current financial situation. Gather all financial documents, including bank statements, credit card bills, and any other records of income and expenses. This comprehensive overview will provide a clear picture of where you stand and what needs to be addressed.

Next, create a realistic budget that reflects your new circumstances. Prioritize essential expenses such as housing, utilities, food, and healthcare. Eliminate or reduce non-essential expenditures, and focus on building an emergency fund. This fund will serve as a financial cushion, helping you navigate unexpected expenses without falling back into financial dependence on your toxic partner.

A crucial aspect of financial independence is generating your own income. If you are currently unemployed or underemployed, consider seeking employment opportunities that align with your skills and interests. Update your resume, network with professionals in your field, and take advantage of job placement services and career counseling. Even part-time or freelance work can provide a valuable source of income and help build your confidence and professional network.

Education and skill-building are powerful tools in your journey towards financial independence. Enroll in courses or training programs that can enhance your qualifications and open doors to better job opportunities. Many community colleges and online platforms offer affordable or even free courses in a wide range of subjects. Investing in your education is an investment in your future, increasing your earning potential and providing a pathway to a more secure and fulfilling life.

Managing debt is another critical component of financial independence. High levels of debt can be overwhelming and may hinder your ability to achieve financial stability. Develop a debt repayment plan that prioritizes high-interest debts and gradually works towards paying off all outstanding balances. Seek advice from financial advisors or credit counseling services if needed, as they can provide guidance and support in managing and reducing debt.

Building a support network is equally important. Surround yourself with friends, family, and professionals who can offer emotional and practical support. Financial independence does not mean you have to navigate this journey alone. Lean on your support network for advice, encouragement, and assistance as you work towards your goals.

Lastly, remember that financial independence is a continuous process. It requires discipline, perseverance, and a commitment to making informed financial decisions. Celebrate your progress, no matter how small, and remain focused on the ultimate goal of achieving a life free from the constraints of a toxic marriage. By taking control of your finances, you are taking a vital step towards a brighter, more empowered future.

Legal Considerations

When contemplating the daunting decision to leave a toxic marriage, one cannot ignore the crucial role that legal considerations play in this life-altering process. It is not merely a matter of walking away; it is about ensuring that you and your children, if you have any, are protected and that your rights are upheld. Legal procedures and protections are designed to help you navigate this turbulent phase with a semblance of stability and security. Ignoring these aspects can lead to dire consequences, potentially exacerbating your already precarious situation.

First and foremost, understanding your legal rights is imperative. Many individuals in toxic marriages feel powerless, their self-esteem eroded by years of emotional or physical abuse. However, knowledge is power. Familiarizing yourself with your state's divorce laws, property division, and child custody regulations can provide you with a sense of control and direction. Consulting with a competent family law attorney can demystify the complexities of the legal system, offering you a tailored strategy to safeguard your interests.

Moreover, documentation cannot be overstressed. In a toxic marriage, your partner may resort to deceitful tactics to manipulate the legal process in their favor. Keeping meticulous records of all interactions, financial transactions, and instances of abuse can serve as invaluable evidence in court. This evidence can substantiate your claims and counter any false allegations made by your spouse. The importance of this cannot be underestimated; it can be the difference between a favorable and unfavorable outcome in your case.

Legal considerations also encompass financial planning. Divorce can be financially draining, and without a clear understanding of your monetary standing, you risk being blindsided by unforeseen expenses. Inventorying all assets and liabilities, understanding spousal support laws, and planning for post-divorce financial independence are all critical steps. Engaging a financial advisor who specializes in divorce can provide you with a realistic picture of your financial health, ensuring that you are not left destitute after the separation.

Child custody is another pivotal legal aspect that requires careful consideration. In toxic marriages, children often become pawns in a bitter battle between spouses. Courts prioritize the best interests of the child, but presenting a compelling case requires more than just good intentions. Detailed records of your involvement in your children's lives, evidence of your spouse's toxic behavior, and a well-thought-out parenting plan are essential. An experienced attorney can guide you through this process, helping you to present a robust case that maximizes your chances of securing favorable custody arrangements.

Lastly, legal protections such as restraining orders can provide immediate relief from an abusive spouse. These orders can offer you and your children a buffer of safety, preventing further harassment or violence. It is crucial to understand how to obtain such orders and the evidence required to support your application. Your attorney can assist you in this, ensuring that you and your loved ones are shielded from immediate harm.

Ignoring legal considerations is not an option when escaping a toxic marriage. It is a multifaceted process that demands careful planning, documentation, and professional guidance. By taking these steps, you not only protect yourself and your children but also lay the groundwork for a new chapter of life, free from the chains of a toxic relationship.

Self-Care Strategies

When the weight of a toxic marriage presses down on your shoulders, it becomes crucial to prioritize yourself. The relentless emotional strain and mental exhaustion can erode your sense of self and well-being. It's vital to recognize that self-care is not a luxury but a necessity, a lifeline that can pull you out of the depths of despair and guide you toward a path of healing and empowerment.

Imagine yourself as a vessel, continuously pouring out your energy, love, and patience without ever replenishing it. Eventually, you become empty, unable to give or even sustain yourself. This is where self-care steps in. It is the act of refilling your vessel, nurturing your mind, body, and soul so that you can regain your strength and clarity. By prioritizing self-care, you start the process of reclaiming your identity and fortifying your resilience against the toxicity that surrounds you.

Establishing a routine that includes activities that bring you joy and relaxation is a powerful first step. Whether it's a morning jog, a quiet moment with a book, or a hobby that you've neglected, these activities are not mere distractions. They are essential to rediscovering your passions and interests, which have likely been overshadowed by the turmoil of your marriage. These moments of self-indulgence are not selfish; they are acts of self-preservation.

Physical health often takes a backseat in the chaos of a toxic relationship. However, neglecting your body can exacerbate the stress and emotional pain you're already enduring. Regular exercise, a balanced diet, and adequate sleep are foundational to your well-being. Exercise, in particular, releases endorphins, which can elevate your mood and provide a much-needed escape from the emotional turbulence. Nourishing your body with healthy food and ensuring you get enough rest will enhance your ability to think clearly and make sound decisions.

Mental and emotional self-care are equally important. Toxic relationships often leave you questioning your sanity and self-worth. Engaging in mindfulness practices, such as meditation or deep-breathing exercises, can help ground you in the present moment and reduce anxiety. Therapy or counseling can provide a safe space to express your feelings and gain perspective. Speaking with a professional can also equip you with strategies to cope with the emotional manipulation and control that often accompany toxic marriages.

Building a support network is another critical aspect of self-care. Isolation is a common tactic in toxic relationships, making you feel alone and helpless. Reaching out to trusted friends and family members can provide the emotional support and validation you need. Sharing your experiences with others who have faced similar situations can also be incredibly empowering. Online forums and support groups can offer a sense of community and understanding, reminding you that you are not alone in this struggle.

Practicing self-compassion is perhaps the most challenging yet most transformative form of self-care. It's easy to fall into the trap of self-blame and guilt, believing that you are somehow responsible for the dysfunction in your marriage. Remind yourself that you deserve kindness and forgiveness, just as you would offer to a dear friend in a similar situation. Allow yourself to feel and process your emotions without judgment.

Self-care is not a one-time act but a continuous commitment to yourself. It is the beacon that guides you through the darkness, illuminating the path toward freedom and healing. By dedicating time and effort to nurture your well-being, you empower yourself to break free from the chains of a toxic marriage and reclaim the life you deserve.

Chapter 6:
The Journey of Healing

Emotional Healing

Imagine waking up every morning feeling as though you're suffocating under the weight of a relationship that drains your spirit and crushes your dreams. A toxic marriage is not just a challenging phase; it's a relentless storm that leaves you feeling isolated, anxious, and emotionally battered. It's time to reclaim your life, your happiness, and most importantly, your emotional well-being.

The first step in this transformative process is acknowledging that your feelings are valid. It's common to second-guess yourself in a toxic relationship, but your pain, your sadness, and your frustration are real. These emotions are your mind's way of signaling that something is fundamentally wrong, and they should not be ignored or dismissed. Recognizing the legitimacy of your feelings is crucial, as it sets the foundation for the healing that must follow.

Next, consider the power of self-reflection. In the chaos of a toxic marriage, it's easy to lose sight of who you are and what you need. Take time to rediscover your passions, your strengths, and your values. Write them down, speak them out loud, or share them with a trusted friend or therapist. This exercise is not about dwelling on the past but about reclaiming your identity and setting a clear vision for your future.

Building a support network is another essential step. Toxic relationships often isolate you from friends and family, leaving you feeling alone and unsupported. Reach out to those who care about you and let them in. Surround yourself with people who uplift you, who listen without judgment, and who genuinely want to see you thrive. Their encouragement and understanding can be a lifeline as you navigate the complexities of emotional recovery.

Mindfulness and self-care are indispensable tools in your healing arsenal. Engaging in activities that bring you peace and joy can counteract the negative effects of a toxic relationship. Whether it's through meditation, exercise, reading, or any hobby that enriches your soul, make time for these practices. They are not luxuries; they are necessities that help rebuild your emotional resilience.

Therapy can also play a pivotal role in your healing journey. A skilled therapist can provide you with strategies to cope with the emotional turmoil and offer you a safe space to express your thoughts and feelings. Therapy can help you unpack the layers of emotional damage and equip you with the skills needed to move forward with confidence and clarity.

Lastly, practice forgiveness—not for your partner, but for yourself. It's easy to fall into the trap of self-blame, wondering what you could have done differently. Understand that you did the best you could with the knowledge and resources you had at the time. Forgiving yourself is an act of kindness that allows you to let go of guilt and shame, making room for healing and growth.

Emotional healing is not a linear process, and it's not something that happens overnight. It requires patience, persistence, and a deep commitment to yourself. But with each step you take, you move closer to breaking free from the chains of a toxic marriage and stepping into a life filled with possibility, peace, and genuine happiness.

Therapy and Counseling

Imagine a life where you wake up each morning feeling valued, respected, and genuinely happy. Picture yourself shedding the heavy chains of a toxic marriage, breathing freely, and stepping into a world where you are empowered to thrive. This transformation is not just a distant dream; it is an attainable reality, and therapy and counseling hold the key to unlocking it.

Therapy and counseling provide a safe space for you to explore the depths of your feelings and experiences. They offer an environment where your voice is heard, your pain acknowledged, and your journey towards healing begins. It's a sanctuary where you can unburden yourself from the emotional baggage that a toxic relationship has thrust upon you. This is not merely about talking; it's about rediscovering your self-worth and reclaiming your life.

When you engage with a qualified therapist, you are taking a proactive step towards mental and emotional liberation. These professionals are trained to help you understand the dynamics of your toxic marriage, identify patterns of behavior, and develop strategies to break free from them. They guide you through the process of self-discovery, helping you to recognize your strengths and build resilience. The insights you gain in therapy can be transformative, offering clarity and a renewed sense of purpose.

Moreover, therapy is not just about addressing the immediate pain; it's about long-term healing and growth. It equips you with tools to manage stress, cope with anxiety, and rebuild your confidence. You learn to set healthy boundaries and develop healthier relationships in the future. The benefits extend beyond your personal life, influencing your professional life and overall well-being. Imagine the impact on your daily interactions when you are no longer weighed down by the toxicity of your past.

Counseling offers a different but equally powerful avenue for support. It often provides a more structured approach to addressing specific issues within your marriage. Whether it's understanding the root causes of conflict, improving communication skills, or navigating the complexities of separation, counseling offers practical solutions. It's a collaborative process where you work with a counselor to set goals and create a plan to achieve them. This focused approach can expedite your journey towards a healthier, happier life.

Group therapy and support groups are additional resources that can be incredibly beneficial. They offer a sense of community and shared experience that can be profoundly comforting. Knowing that you are not alone, that others have walked a similar path and emerged stronger, can be a powerful motivator. These groups provide not only emotional support but also practical advice and strategies from those who have successfully navigated their own toxic relationships.

Investing in therapy and counseling is an investment in yourself. It's an affirmation that your well-being matters, that you deserve to live a life free from the shadows of a toxic marriage. It's about taking control, making empowered choices, and moving towards a future filled with possibilities. Don't let fear or uncertainty hold you back. Reach out, seek the help you need, and take the first step towards breaking free from the chains that bind you. Your journey to a brighter, healthier, and more fulfilling life starts now.

Coping Mechanisms

When entangled in the snares of a toxic marriage, finding a way to cope can feel like navigating through a dense fog. However, adopting effective coping mechanisms is not just a means of survival; it is a path to empowerment and eventual liberation. The first step in this transformative process is recognizing the importance of self-care. Prioritizing your physical and mental well-being is essential. Begin by ensuring you have a support system in place—friends, family, or a therapist—someone who can provide the emotional backing you need.

Imagine the relief of pouring your heart out to someone who understands your plight without judgment. This emotional release can act as a pressure valve, reducing the overwhelming stress that often accompanies a toxic relationship. Furthermore, engaging in physical activities such as yoga, jogging, or even a simple walk in the park can work wonders. These activities not only improve your physical health but also serve as a mental escape, allowing you to clear your mind and regain focus.

Another powerful coping strategy is setting boundaries. In a toxic marriage, boundaries often become blurred, leading to emotional exhaustion. Establishing clear, firm boundaries can act as a protective shield, reducing the frequency and intensity of negative interactions. Communicate your limits assertively but calmly, and hold your ground. This act of self-respect can diminish the toxic influence your partner has over you, fostering a sense of autonomy and control.

Journaling is another invaluable tool. Putting your thoughts and feelings down on paper can provide clarity and insight into your situation. This practice enables you to track patterns of behavior, both yours and your partner's, which can be crucial for planning your next steps. Moreover, journaling can act as a confidential space where you can express your fears, hopes, and plans without the risk of external judgment.

Engaging in mindfulness and meditation practices can also offer significant benefits. These techniques help you stay present, reducing anxiety and preventing your mind from spiraling into worst-case scenarios. Mindfulness can empower you to respond to situations more thoughtfully rather than reacting impulsively, which is often a trigger in toxic dynamics.

Financial independence is another critical aspect of coping. Ensuring you have your own financial resources can provide a sense of security and open up options for the future. Whether it's saving money, pursuing a new job, or acquiring new skills, financial independence can act as a lifeline, offering you the freedom to make decisions that are in your best interest.

Lastly, never underestimate the power of seeking professional help. Therapists and counselors are trained to guide you through tumultuous times, offering strategies and insights that you might not have considered. They can provide a neutral perspective, helping you to see the bigger picture and assess your options more clearly.

By incorporating these coping mechanisms into your daily life, you can transform your existence from one of mere survival to one of strength and resilience. These strategies not only help you manage the immediate stressors but also pave the way for long-term healing and empowerment. Taking these steps is not just about escaping a toxic marriage; it's about reclaiming your life.

Finding Your Strength

Liberating yourself from a toxic marriage is not merely about leaving a harmful relationship; it's about rediscovering the powerful individual that lies within you. Every person possesses an inner reservoir of strength, a wellspring of resilience that often goes untapped. In the context of a toxic marriage, this strength can become buried under layers of emotional turmoil, self-doubt, and fear. But it is there, waiting to be unearthed and harnessed.

Recognizing this strength begins with acknowledging your worth. For too long, a toxic marriage may have eroded your sense of self, making you question your value and capabilities. It's crucial to affirm, and continually remind yourself, that you are deserving of love, respect, and happiness. Self-worth is not something bestowed upon us by others; it is an intrinsic quality that we must reclaim for ourselves. Stand in front of a mirror and speak words of affirmation. Tell yourself that you are strong, capable, and deserving of better. This simple act can ignite a powerful shift in your mindset.

Next, reflect on your past achievements and challenges you've overcome. These moments are testaments to your resilience. Whether it was excelling in a career, nurturing a friendship through tough times, or managing daily life with grace under pressure, these instances are proof of your inner strength. Write them down, celebrate them, and let them serve as reminders of what you are capable of achieving.

Reconnecting with your passions and interests is another vital step. Toxic relationships often suffocate personal growth and stifle individual pursuits. Reignite your passions, whether they are hobbies, professional goals, or creative endeavors. Engaging in activities that bring you joy and fulfillment can be incredibly empowering. They not only provide a sense of purpose but also rebuild your confidence, reminding you of the vibrant individual you are outside the confines of a toxic relationship.

It's also essential to surround yourself with a supportive network. Friends, family, and support groups can provide the encouragement and reinforcement needed to bolster your strength. These connections remind you that you are not alone and that there are people who believe in you and your journey towards a healthier life. Lean on them when needed, and allow their strength to fuel your own.

Mindfulness and self-care practices play a pivotal role in fortifying your strength. Engage in activities that promote mental and emotional well-being, such as meditation, yoga, or journaling. These practices help in grounding your thoughts, reducing anxiety, and fostering a sense of inner peace. Taking care of your mental health is not just about coping with the present but also about building resilience for the future.

Lastly, seek professional guidance if needed. Therapists and counselors can provide invaluable tools and strategies to help you navigate this challenging transition. They can offer a safe space to process your emotions, gain clarity, and develop a plan for moving forward. Professional support is not a sign of weakness but a step towards empowerment and self-discovery.

Rediscovering your strength is a transformative process. It's about peeling back the layers of doubt and fear imposed by a toxic marriage and unveiling the confident, capable individual that you are. By affirming your worth, celebrating your resilience, reconnecting with your passions, building a supportive network, practicing mindfulness, and seeking professional guidance, you can reclaim your strength. This newfound strength will not only help you break free from the chains of a toxic marriage but also pave the way for a future filled with hope, self-assurance, and boundless potential.

Rebuilding Your Identity

Breaking free from the grip of a toxic marriage is a monumental step, but the next crucial phase is reconstructing the shattered pieces of your identity. Years spent in a relationship that eroded your sense of self can leave you feeling lost and unsure of who you truly are. It's time to reclaim your life and redefine your essence.

First, understand that you are more than the sum of your past experiences. Toxic relationships often distort your self-perception, convincing you that you are less than you are. These negative narratives are not the truth. You possess inherent worth and potential that were merely obscured by the toxicity. Begin by acknowledging your strengths and achievements, no matter how small they may seem. Write them down, celebrate them, and let them remind you of your capability and resilience.

Next, reconnect with your passions and interests. What activities used to bring you joy before the relationship dulled your enthusiasm? Whether it's painting, hiking, reading, or dancing, immerse yourself in pursuits that reignite your spirit. These hobbies are not just pastimes; they are pathways to rediscovering your true self. Engage in them regularly, and watch as they help rebuild your confidence and zest for life.

Building a support network is another vital step. Surround yourself with individuals who uplift and encourage you. Friends, family, support groups, or therapists can provide the emotional sustenance necessary for healing. These connections serve as a mirror, reflecting your worth back to you when you struggle to see it yourself. They also offer a safe space to express your feelings and fears, helping you process and move beyond the trauma.

Setting new goals can also propel you forward. Reflect on what you want to achieve in this new chapter of your life. These goals can be as ambitious as starting a new career or as simple as cultivating a daily mindfulness practice. The act of setting and working towards goals fosters a sense of purpose and direction, essential components of a healthy identity.

Self-compassion is paramount. The aftermath of a toxic marriage often leaves emotional scars that can trigger self-doubt and criticism. Practice kindness towards yourself. Understand that healing is not linear and setbacks are part of the journey. Treat yourself with the same empathy and patience you would offer a dear friend. This gentleness nurtures your wounded self-esteem and fosters a nurturing internal environment where your true identity can flourish.

Lastly, give yourself permission to redefine your life on your terms. Society often imposes rigid roles and expectations, but your journey is unique. Embrace the freedom to explore different facets of yourself without guilt or fear. Experiment with new styles, ideas, and lifestyles. This experimentation is not an act of rebellion but an essential process of self-discovery.

Rebuilding your identity after a toxic marriage is an empowering endeavor. It requires courage, patience, and a commitment to self-love. By recognizing your worth, reconnecting with your passions, building a supportive network, setting new goals, practicing self-compassion, and exploring new possibilities, you can emerge stronger and more authentically yourself. Your past does not define you; your actions today do. Seize this opportunity to craft a life that reflects your true essence and potential.

Chapter 7:
The Power of Self-Love

Understanding Self-Love

In the throes of a toxic marriage, one can lose sight of the most vital relationship of all—the relationship with oneself. For too long, the focus has been on pleasing a partner, fixing a broken bond, or merely surviving the day-to-day turmoil. But now, it's time to redirect that energy inward and cultivate a profound sense of self-love. This isn't just a fluffy concept; it's a lifeline, a necessity to reclaim your life and your happiness.

Imagine waking up each day with a sense of peace, knowing that your worth isn't tied to another person's validation. Picture yourself making decisions that prioritize your well-being, free from the chains of guilt or obligation. This is what self-love offers. It's the foundation upon which you can rebuild a life of joy and fulfillment, independent of the toxic influences that have overshadowed your existence.

Self-love begins with self-awareness. It's about recognizing your needs, desires, and boundaries. In the chaos of a toxic relationship, these essential aspects of yourself have likely been neglected or dismissed. But they matter. You matter. Start by taking a moment each day to check in with yourself. What are you feeling? What do you need? These questions might seem simple, but they are powerful tools for reclaiming your sense of self.

Furthermore, self-love involves self-compassion. It's easy to fall into the trap of self-blame, especially when a relationship turns sour. But the truth is, no one deserves to be treated poorly, and that includes you. Be kind to yourself. Acknowledge the pain you've endured and give yourself permission to heal. This isn't about excusing any harmful behavior from your partner; it's about recognizing that you deserve better and treating yourself with the same kindness and respect you would offer a dear friend.

Setting boundaries is another crucial aspect of self-love. In a toxic marriage, boundaries are often blurred or outright ignored. Reclaiming your life means establishing clear limits on what is acceptable and what is not. This might mean saying no to certain behaviors, demanding respect, or even making the difficult decision to leave the relationship altogether. Boundaries are not about building walls; they're about creating a safe space where you can thrive.

Investing in self-care is equally important. This isn't just about pampering yourself, although that can be a part of it. True self-care involves nurturing your physical, emotional, and mental well-being. Exercise, eat well, and get enough sleep. Seek therapy or counseling if you need it. Engage in activities that bring you joy and fulfillment. By taking care of yourself, you reinforce the message that you are worthy of love and respect.

Lastly, surround yourself with positive influences. Toxic relationships often isolate you from friends and family who could offer support. Reconnecting with these people can provide a much-needed sense of community and belonging. Their encouragement and love can serve as a powerful reminder that you are not alone and that you deserve happiness.

Self-love is not a luxury; it's a necessity. It's the first and most crucial step towards escaping the chains of a toxic marriage and reclaiming your life. By fostering self-awareness, self-compassion, and self-care, you lay the groundwork for a brighter, healthier future. And remember, you are worthy of love—not just from others, but from yourself.

Building Self-Esteem

A toxic marriage can be an overwhelming, soul-crushing experience that leaves you questioning your worth and abilities. When you are constantly belittled, manipulated, or controlled, it's all too easy to lose sight of your own value. Rebuilding your self-esteem is not just a step toward healing; it's an essential act of reclaiming your life and identity.

Imagine the freedom of waking up each day without the weight of constant criticism and judgment. Picture the strength in your eyes when you look in the mirror and see someone who is worthy of love and respect, someone who is capable of achieving great things. This is not a distant fantasy but a reachable reality. The path to self-esteem is paved with small, deliberate actions and a commitment to valuing yourself above the toxic voices that once dominated your life.

First and foremost, recognize that your worth is intrinsic. No one has the right to diminish your value. The negative narrative imposed upon you in a toxic marriage is a reflection of the other person's insecurities and manipulations, not of your true self. Begin by challenging these falsehoods. Write down the negative statements you've been told and counter them with positive affirmations. For every "You're not good enough," respond with "I am capable and deserving." Repetition of these affirmations will start to rewire your brain, replacing the toxic messages with empowering truths.

Next, take stock of your accomplishments and strengths. Often, we overlook our own achievements because we've been conditioned to minimize them. Make a list of everything you've done that makes you proud, no matter how small. Did you complete a project at work? Did you help a friend in need? Celebrate these victories. They are evidence of your competence and kindness, traits that a toxic partner would have you believe are non-existent.

Surround yourself with positivity. Toxic marriages isolate you from supportive friends and family, making you feel alone and helpless. Reconnect with those who uplift you and see your worth. Their encouragement can serve as a mirror reflecting your true value. Join groups or communities that share your interests and values, where you can form new, healthy relationships. The more you engage with positive influences, the more you will begin to internalize their affirmations.

Engage in self-care practices that reinforce your worth. Exercise, healthy eating, and adequate sleep are fundamental, but also indulge in activities that bring you joy and relaxation. Read books, take long baths, meditate, or pursue hobbies that you love. These acts of self-care are declarations of your worthiness to yourself and the world.

Set boundaries. One of the most damaging aspects of a toxic marriage is the erosion of personal boundaries. Reestablishing these boundaries is crucial for your self-esteem. Learn to say no without guilt. Protect your time and energy from those who drain it. This is not selfish; it's necessary for your well-being.

Seek professional help if needed. Therapists and counselors can provide invaluable guidance and tools for rebuilding self-esteem. They can help you navigate the complex emotions and trauma that come from a toxic marriage, offering strategies tailored to your unique situation.

Reclaiming your self-esteem is a powerful act of defiance against the toxicity that sought to diminish you. It's a declaration that you are worthy of respect, love, and happiness. It's the foundation upon which you will rebuild your life, stronger and more resilient than ever before. The chains of a toxic marriage may have held you down, but they do not define you. Your true worth is waiting to be rediscovered, and the power to do so lies within you.

Setting Boundaries

In the labyrinth of a toxic marriage, establishing boundaries is not just a necessity; it is a lifeline. Boundaries are the demarcation lines that protect your mental, emotional, and physical well-being. Without them, you become vulnerable to manipulation, control, and emotional abuse. Imagine yourself as a fortress; boundaries are the walls that shield you from the relentless onslaught of negativity and toxicity.

Many individuals trapped in toxic marriages often struggle with the concept of boundaries. They fear that setting limits will escalate conflicts or lead to further isolation. However, the reality is quite the opposite. Boundaries are not walls that imprison; they are gates that allow you to reclaim your autonomy and self-worth. They are the ultimate act of self-respect and self-love.

Consider the power dynamics at play in a toxic marriage. The toxic partner often thrives on control and manipulation, eroding your sense of self. By setting boundaries, you disrupt this dynamic. You send a clear message that your needs and well-being are non-negotiable. This shift in power can be a catalyst for change, forcing the toxic partner to confront their behavior or risk losing their grip on you.

Establishing boundaries requires clarity and conviction. Begin by identifying what behaviors are unacceptable and detrimental to your well-being. Is it constant criticism, emotional blackmail, or physical intimidation? Whatever the toxic patterns may be, recognize them and articulate your limits. Communicate your boundaries assertively and without apology. Use "I" statements to express how certain behaviors affect you and what you will no longer tolerate.

For example, you might say, "I feel disrespected when my opinions are dismissed. I need my viewpoints to be considered and valued." This approach does not attack the other person but rather emphasizes your feelings and needs. It is a powerful way to assert your boundaries while maintaining a level of respect and dignity.

Enforcing boundaries is equally crucial. It is not enough to merely state them; you must also follow through with consequences if they are violated. Consequences are not about punishment but about protecting your well-being. They reinforce the importance of your boundaries and demonstrate that you are serious about maintaining them. If a boundary is crossed, calmly and firmly implement the agreed-upon consequence. This might mean taking a break from a conversation, seeking therapy, or even considering separation if the toxicity persists.

Self-care is an integral part of setting boundaries. It fortifies you against the emotional toll of a toxic marriage and empowers you to uphold your limits. Engage in activities that nurture your soul, whether it's spending time with supportive friends, pursuing hobbies, or practicing mindfulness. Self-care replenishes your strength and reminds you of your inherent worth, making it easier to stand firm in your boundaries.

Remember, setting boundaries is not an act of selfishness; it is an act of survival. It is about creating a safe space for yourself where you can heal, grow, and thrive. Boundaries are the foundation upon which you build a life free from the chains of toxicity. They are your declaration of independence, your commitment to a healthier, more fulfilling existence.

Take the first step today. Define your boundaries, communicate them clearly, and uphold them steadfastly. Your well-being depends on it.

Positive Affirmations

Imagine waking up each day with a renewed sense of purpose, a feeling of worthiness, and a belief that you are capable of achieving anything. This is not a distant dream or a fantasy; it is a reality waiting to be unlocked through the power of positive affirmations. In the midst of a toxic marriage, it is easy to lose sight of your self-worth and potential. Negative words and actions can erode your confidence, leaving you feeling trapped and powerless. However, the practice of positive affirmations can be a transformative tool to rebuild your self-esteem and reclaim your life.

Positive affirmations are simple yet powerful statements that you repeat to yourself to challenge and overcome self-sabotaging and negative thoughts. They are a form of self-empowerment that can reshape your mental landscape, fostering a mindset of strength and resilience. By consistently affirming your value, capabilities, and right to happiness, you can counteract the damaging effects of a toxic relationship.

Consider the impact of hearing negative comments day in and day out. Over time, these words can become internalized, shaping your self-perception and limiting your potential. Now, imagine the opposite: hearing and believing positive statements about yourself regularly. This shift in internal dialogue can significantly alter your emotional state and overall well-being. Positive affirmations act as a counterbalance to the negativity, helping you to build a new narrative about who you are and what you can achieve.

To integrate positive affirmations into your daily routine, start by identifying areas where you feel the most vulnerable or insecure. These are the aspects of your life where affirmations can have the most profound impact. For example, if you struggle with self-worth, an affirmation such as "I am worthy of love and respect" can be incredibly powerful. If you feel powerless, "I have the strength to change my life" can serve as a daily reminder of your inner resilience.

The key to effective affirmations is consistency. Make it a habit to repeat your chosen affirmations multiple times a day, especially during moments of doubt or stress. Write them down and place them where you can see them frequently – on your bathroom mirror, your computer screen, or even as a reminder on your phone. The more you repeat and believe these statements, the more they will become ingrained in your psyche, gradually replacing negative thoughts with positive ones.

Moreover, positive affirmations can serve as a catalyst for action. When you start to believe in your worth and capabilities, you are more likely to take steps towards improving your situation. Affirmations can motivate you to seek support, set boundaries, and make decisions that align with your well-being. They empower you to envision a future where you are not defined by the toxicity of your marriage but by your strength and potential.

Incorporating positive affirmations into your life is not just about repeating words; it's about fostering a mindset that propels you towards healing and growth. It is about reclaiming your narrative and recognizing that you have the power to create a life filled with joy, respect, and fulfillment. By embracing positive affirmations, you take a crucial step towards breaking free from the chains of a toxic marriage and building a future that reflects your true worth.

The Art of Saying No

In the labyrinth of a toxic marriage, the power of a single word can become your greatest ally: "No." It's not just a word; it's a declaration of self-worth, a boundary that signifies your refusal to be diminished or manipulated. Many individuals find themselves ensnared in a cycle of compliance, fearing that saying "no" will escalate conflicts or lead to emotional or physical repercussions. However, the art of saying no is an essential skill for reclaiming your autonomy and dignity.

Imagine a scenario where your partner insists on making decisions that solely benefit them, disregarding your needs and desires. By acquiescing, you inadvertently reinforce their behavior, perpetuating a toxic dynamic. Saying no disrupts this cycle, forcing a reevaluation of the relationship's power structure. It communicates that your voice matters, that your consent is not a given but a privilege to be earned.

The first step in mastering this art is to recognize your right to say no. It's crucial to internalize that your needs and boundaries are valid. Many people in toxic marriages have been conditioned to prioritize their partner's demands over their own well-being. This conditioning can make the act of saying no feel like an insurmountable challenge. Yet, it is precisely this act that can begin to unravel the chains that bind you.

Effective communication is key. Saying no doesn't have to be confrontational. It can be a calm, assertive statement that leaves no room for misinterpretation. Practice phrases like, "I am not comfortable with this," or "This doesn't work for me." These statements are clear and respectful, yet firm. They convey your stance without aggression, reducing the likelihood of an explosive reaction from your partner.

Understand that saying no may initially provoke resistance or backlash. Toxic partners often rely on manipulation and control, and your newfound assertiveness can be perceived as a threat. Stand your ground. The initial discomfort is a small price to pay for long-term liberation. Over time, consistent boundaries can lead to a shift in the relationship's dynamics. Your partner may begin to understand that their behavior is unacceptable, or you may gain the clarity needed to make more significant decisions about your future.

Support systems play a vital role in this journey. Surround yourself with friends, family, or support groups who understand your situation and can offer encouragement and advice. Their perspectives can provide the strength and clarity needed to uphold your boundaries. Professional counseling can also be invaluable, offering strategies tailored to your specific circumstances.

Remember, saying no is not an act of selfishness; it is an act of self-preservation. It is a way to protect your mental, emotional, and sometimes physical health. It is a statement that you deserve respect and consideration. In a toxic marriage, where your sense of self can be continually eroded, reclaiming the power to say no is a crucial step towards rebuilding your identity and self-esteem.

The art of saying no is a skill that, once mastered, can transform not only your relationship but your entire life. It is the cornerstone of self-respect and the foundation upon which you can build a healthier, more fulfilling existence.

Chapter 8:
Finding Happiness After Toxicity

Rediscovering Joy

Imagine a life where every day feels like a breath of fresh air, where your heart is lighter, and your spirit soars with newfound freedom. This is not a distant dream but an achievable reality. Escaping the chains of a toxic marriage is not just about leaving behind the negativity; it is about rediscovering the joy that has long been buried under layers of pain and suffering.

A toxic marriage can drain the very essence of who you are, leaving you feeling empty and devoid of happiness. The constant emotional turmoil, the never-ending arguments, and the pervasive sense of hopelessness can take a toll on your mental and physical well-being. However, breaking free from such a relationship is the first step towards reclaiming your life and finding the joy that you deserve.

Rediscovering joy begins with the simple yet profound act of self-care. For too long, you may have neglected your own needs, prioritizing the demands of a toxic partner. Now is the time to turn the focus inward. Engage in activities that bring you pleasure and fulfillment, whether it's a hobby you once loved, spending time with supportive friends, or simply taking a moment each day to breathe and reflect. Self-care is not a luxury; it is a necessity for healing and rejuvenation.

Another crucial aspect of finding joy is to reconnect with your passions and interests. Toxic relationships often stifle personal growth and creativity. Reclaiming your individuality involves exploring new opportunities and rediscovering old interests that once brought you happiness. Take a class, join a club, or volunteer for a cause that resonates with you. These activities not only provide a sense of purpose but also open doors to new friendships and experiences.

Surrounding yourself with positive influences is equally important. Toxic relationships can isolate you from friends and family, leaving you feeling alone and unsupported. Rebuilding these connections is vital for your emotional health. Reach out to loved ones who genuinely care about your well-being. Share your journey with them and allow their encouragement to uplift and inspire you. Positive relationships act as a buffer against the lingering effects of a toxic marriage, helping you to rebuild your confidence and self-worth.

Setting boundaries is another essential step in rediscovering joy. A toxic marriage often involves a lack of respect for personal boundaries, leading to feelings of helplessness and frustration. As you move forward, it is crucial to establish clear and healthy boundaries in all aspects of your life. This means learning to say no without guilt, protecting your time and energy, and ensuring that your needs are met. Boundaries empower you to take control of your life and create a safe space for yourself.

Lastly, practicing gratitude can significantly enhance your sense of joy. It may seem challenging to find things to be grateful for after enduring a toxic relationship, but even small acts of appreciation can have a profound impact on your outlook. Keep a gratitude journal, noting down moments of joy and positivity each day. Over time, this practice helps shift your focus from the negative experiences of the past to the positive possibilities of the future.

By prioritizing self-care, reconnecting with passions, surrounding yourself with positivity, setting boundaries, and practicing gratitude, you open the door to a life filled with joy and fulfillment. Breaking free from a toxic marriage is not just an escape; it is a powerful step towards rediscovering the happiness that has always been within your reach.

Embracing Solitude

Leaving a toxic marriage is an act of bravery, a step towards reclaiming one's life from the clutches of emotional and mental torment. The fear of loneliness often paralyzes individuals, chaining them to their suffering. However, solitude should not be viewed as a void, but as an opportunity for growth, self-discovery, and healing. To break free from the shackles of a destructive relationship, one must redefine the concept of being alone.

Solitude is not synonymous with isolation. It provides a sanctuary where one can reflect on one's experiences, understand one's emotions, and rediscover one's true self. In the quiet moments of being alone, there is a chance to listen to the inner voice that was silenced by years of manipulation and control. This voice, often ignored or suppressed, holds the key to personal truth and authenticity.

The liberation from a toxic marriage is the first step towards nurturing a healthier relationship with oneself. This newfound freedom allows individuals to set boundaries, prioritize their needs, and cultivate self-love. It is a time to explore personal interests and passions that were neglected or sacrificed. Engaging in activities that bring joy and fulfillment can reignite a sense of purpose and self-worth.

Moreover, solitude offers a space to process grief and loss. The end of a marriage, even a toxic one, involves mourning the loss of what could have been. This grieving process is crucial as it allows for the release of pent-up emotions and fosters emotional resilience. Through solitude, one can confront one's pain, acknowledge it, and ultimately, heal from it.

Building a support system is essential during this period. While solitude is valuable, human connection remains a fundamental need. Surrounding oneself with supportive friends and family can provide the encouragement and affirmation needed to navigate this challenging transition. Additionally, seeking professional help from therapists or support groups can offer guidance and tools to cope with the emotional aftermath of a toxic marriage.

Solitude also presents an opportunity to redefine personal values and goals. Without the influence of a toxic partner, individuals can reassess what is truly important to them. This reflection can lead to the establishment of new, healthier relationships and a life aligned with one's true desires and aspirations.

The path to self-discovery is not without its challenges. There will be moments of doubt, fear, and loneliness. However, these moments are temporary and part of the healing process. Each step taken in solitude is a step towards empowerment and self-sufficiency. It is an investment in one's future, paving the way for a life free from the shadows of a toxic past.

Choosing to embrace solitude is a powerful act of self-love and respect. It signifies a commitment to oneself and a refusal to settle for anything less than what one deserves. By embracing solitude, individuals can transform their lives, reclaim their identity, and ultimately, find peace and happiness within themselves.

Creating a Life, You Love

Breaking free from a toxic marriage is not just an act of survival; it is a declaration of self-worth and a gateway to a future filled with endless possibilities. Imagine waking up each day with a sense of purpose and joy, rather than the dread and anxiety that once clouded your mornings. This transformation is not merely a dream but a tangible reality that you can create for yourself.

The first step to building a life you truly love is recognizing that you deserve it. For too long, you may have been conditioned to believe that your happiness is secondary, that your needs and desires are less important than maintaining a semblance of peace in a toxic relationship. This is a fallacy that must be shattered. Your happiness is not a luxury; it is a necessity. By acknowledging your right to a fulfilling and joyous life, you lay the foundation for all the positive changes to come.

Next, consider the passions and interests that have been stifled or neglected. What activities make you lose track of time? What subjects ignite a fire within you? Reconnecting with these passions is crucial. They are not mere hobbies or distractions; they are integral components of your identity. They provide a sense of accomplishment and self-worth that is independent of any external validation. Pursuing these interests will not only bring you joy but also serve as a powerful reminder of your capabilities and potential.

Financial independence is another cornerstone of a life you love. Money may not buy happiness, but it certainly provides freedom and security. Whether it's advancing in your current career, acquiring new skills, or even starting your own business, taking control of your financial destiny is empowering. It allows you to make choices based on your desires and values rather than out of necessity or fear.

Relationships are also pivotal. Surround yourself with people who uplift and support you, rather than those who drain your energy or belittle your aspirations. Cultivate friendships that are based on mutual respect and shared values. These relationships will serve as a robust support system, providing encouragement and perspective as you navigate your new path.

Physical and mental health cannot be overlooked. A toxic marriage often takes a toll on your well-being, manifesting as chronic stress, anxiety, or even physical ailments. Prioritize self-care by engaging in regular exercise, maintaining a balanced diet, and seeking professional help if needed. Mental health is equally important; practices such as mindfulness, meditation, or therapy can provide invaluable tools for managing stress and fostering a positive outlook.

Lastly, set clear, achievable goals. These goals serve as milestones on your journey to a fulfilling life. They provide direction and a sense of accomplishment as you achieve them one by one. Whether it's traveling to a dream destination, learning a new skill, or simply enjoying more quality time with loved ones, these goals will keep you motivated and focused.

Creating a life you love is not an overnight transformation but a series of deliberate, empowering choices. Each step you take away from the shadows of a toxic marriage and towards the light of self-fulfillment is a testament to your strength and resilience. This new life is not just possible; it is waiting for you to claim it. Seize it with both hands and never look back.

Pursuing Your Passions

In the aftermath of a toxic marriage, the road to healing is paved with rediscovery and self-empowerment. A critical step in this process is reconnecting with your passions. These are not mere hobbies or pastimes; they are the lifeblood of your individuality, the essence of what makes you unique. They are the pursuits that ignite your spirit and provide a sense of purpose and fulfillment. It is time to reclaim them.

First, identify what you genuinely love. Reflect on what once made your heart race with excitement before the shadows of your relationship dulled your enthusiasm. Was it painting, writing, hiking, or perhaps a musical instrument you used to play? These passions are not lost; they have merely been buried under the weight of your past circumstances. Unearth them and allow yourself the freedom to explore them once more.

Engaging in activities that you are passionate about can serve as a powerful antidote to the emotional scars left by a toxic marriage. These pursuits offer a sanctuary, a haven where you can express yourself freely without judgment or criticism. They provide an opportunity to channel your energy into something positive and constructive. This shift in focus is not just a distraction; it is a form of therapy. It nurtures your mental and emotional well-being, helping you to rebuild your self-esteem and confidence.

Moreover, pursuing your passions can lead to the discovery of new talents and interests. As you immerse yourself in activities that bring you joy, you may find that your abilities extend beyond what you previously imagined. This process of exploration can open doors to new opportunities, friendships, and even career paths. It is about expanding your horizons and allowing yourself to grow in ways that were previously stifled.

It is essential to prioritize these passions in your life. Make a conscious effort to carve out time for them, regardless of how busy your schedule may be. This is not about being selfish; it is about self-care. By dedicating time to what you love, you are investing in your happiness and well-being. This, in turn, benefits those around you, as a happier, more fulfilled version of yourself is better equipped to nurture and support others.

Sharing your passions with others can also be incredibly rewarding. Join clubs, groups, or online communities where you can connect with like-minded individuals. These connections can provide a sense of belonging and support, reinforcing that you are not alone in your journey. They can offer encouragement, inspiration, and even collaboration opportunities, enriching your experience further.

It is important to recognize that pursuing your passions is not a luxury; it is a necessity. In the wake of a toxic marriage, reclaiming your passions is a vital step towards rebuilding your identity and forging a new path forward. It empowers you to take control of your life, to define your own happiness, and to live authentically.

As you move forward, remember that your passions are a reflection of your true self. They are a testament to your resilience and your ability to find joy and meaning despite past hardships. By embracing them, you are not only healing but also celebrating the person you are and the person you are becoming.

Building Healthy Relationships

Imagine a life where your relationships are not a source of stress but a wellspring of joy and fulfillment. For too long, you may have been entangled in a toxic marriage, feeling trapped and suffocated. It's time to break free from these chains and step into a world where healthy relationships flourish and nurture your well-being.

Healthy relationships are built on a foundation of mutual respect, trust, and open communication. These elements are not just desirable; they are essential. Without them, relationships crumble, leaving behind emotional wreckage that takes years to repair. If you have experienced the toxicity of a harmful marriage, you know firsthand the damage that can be done when these critical components are missing. However, the good news is that you have the power to cultivate healthy relationships moving forward.

Respect is the cornerstone of any healthy relationship. It means valuing each other's opinions, feelings, and boundaries. In a toxic marriage, respect is often the first casualty, leading to a breakdown in communication and trust. To build healthier relationships, start by practicing self-respect. Recognize your worth and insist on being treated with dignity. When you respect yourself, you set a standard for how others should treat you.

Trust is another vital ingredient. It is the glue that holds relationships together. Without trust, even the strongest bonds can unravel. In a toxic marriage, trust is often eroded by lies, deceit, and betrayal. Rebuilding trust takes time and effort, but it is possible. Begin by being trustworthy yourself. Be honest, keep your promises, and show that you are reliable. When you are consistent in your actions, others will learn to trust you.

Open communication is the lifeline of a relationship. It involves not just talking but listening—truly listening. In a toxic marriage, communication is often one-sided or filled with negativity. To foster healthy relationships, practice active listening. Pay attention to what the other person is saying without planning your response while they are speaking. Show empathy and understanding. When both parties feel heard and validated, communication becomes a tool for connection rather than conflict.

Healthy relationships also require boundaries. Boundaries are not about keeping people out; they are about protecting your well-being. They define what is acceptable and what is not. In a toxic marriage, boundaries are often violated, leading to feelings of helplessness and resentment. Establishing and maintaining boundaries is crucial for your emotional health. Communicate your boundaries clearly and assertively. Remember, it is okay to say no. Your needs and feelings are just as important as anyone else's.

Another key aspect is shared values and goals. Relationships thrive when both parties are aligned in their vision for the future. In a toxic marriage, conflicting values can create constant tension and discord. Seek relationships with individuals who share your core values and aspirations. This alignment fosters a sense of partnership and mutual support.

Surround yourself with positive influences. Healthy relationships are not limited to romantic ones. Friendships, family connections, and professional relationships all contribute to your overall well-being. Choose to spend time with people who uplift and inspire you. Their positive energy will reinforce your commitment to maintaining healthy relationships.

Breaking free from a toxic marriage is a courageous step towards a better life. By focusing on respect, trust, open communication, boundaries, shared values, and positive influences, you can build relationships that enhance your happiness and personal growth. You deserve relationships that are nourishing and empowering. Take hold of the reins of your life and cultivate the healthy connections you've always dreamed of.

Chapter 9:
Forgiveness and Letting Go

Understanding Forgiveness

Forgiveness is not just a noble concept; it is a vital necessity for anyone seeking to escape the chains of a toxic marriage. The very word "forgiveness" often conjures images of weakness or surrender, yet it is, in truth, an act of immense strength and resilience. It's easy to harbor resentment and anger, to let these emotions fester and poison our spirits. However, the path to healing and liberation from a toxic relationship begins with a conscious decision to forgive.

Forgiveness does not mean condoning the wrongs inflicted upon you or forgetting the pain endured. It means acknowledging the hurt, understanding its impact, and choosing to release the grip it has on your heart. This release is not for the benefit of the one who wronged you; it is for your own peace of mind and emotional freedom. Holding on to bitterness and grudges only prolongs your suffering and keeps you chained to the past.

In a toxic marriage, emotional wounds are often deep and complex. The betrayal, manipulation, and emotional abuse can leave scars that seem impossible to heal. Yet, it is precisely these deep wounds that necessitate the power of forgiveness. By forgiving, you are not absolving your partner of their misdeeds; you are reclaiming your power and refusing to let their actions define your future.

Forgiveness is a deliberate act of self-love. It involves recognizing that you deserve to be free from the emotional shackles that bind you to a painful past. It is about prioritizing your well-being over the desire for retribution. This shift in perspective allows you to focus on your own growth and recovery, rather than being consumed by the actions of another.

The process of forgiveness is not instantaneous; it is a gradual journey that requires patience and self-compassion. It begins with an honest assessment of the hurt and an acceptance of your feelings. Allow yourself to grieve the loss and acknowledge the injustice. This emotional honesty is the first step toward healing.

Next, consider the broader context of your partner's behavior. Understanding the root causes of their actions does not excuse their behavior, but it can provide insight that aids in the forgiveness process. People often act out of their own unresolved pain and insecurities. Recognizing this can help you see them as flawed human beings rather than villains.

Forgiveness also involves setting boundaries and making choices that protect your emotional health. It is not about reconciling or giving the other person another chance to hurt you. It is about freeing yourself from the emotional burden they placed upon you. This empowerment enables you to move forward with clarity and strength, unencumbered by the past.

As you navigate this path, seek support from friends, family, or a therapist. Sharing your experiences and feelings can provide validation and comfort, making the process less isolating. Surround yourself with positivity and people who uplift you, reinforcing your resolve to forgive and move on.

Forgiveness is the key to unlocking the door to a brighter, healthier future. It is an act of courage that breaks the cycle of toxicity and paves the way for genuine healing. By choosing to forgive, you are not only escaping the chains of a toxic marriage but also embracing the possibility of a life filled with peace, joy, and self-empowerment.

The Power of Letting Go

Imagine waking up every day feeling suffocated by an invisible weight, a constant pressure that drains your energy and stifles your spirit. This is the reality of living in a toxic marriage. It's a relentless cycle of emotional turmoil, where hope is a distant memory and peace seems like an unattainable dream. Yet, there is a way to reclaim your life, to rediscover your inner strength and to break free from the chains that bind you. This path begins with the profound act of letting go.

Letting go is not an admission of defeat, but a courageous step toward self-preservation and renewal. It is the recognition that your well-being is paramount, and that staying in a harmful environment only perpetuates your suffering. Toxic marriages thrive on control, manipulation, and emotional abuse, eroding your self-worth and leaving you feeling powerless. By choosing to let go, you are asserting your right to a life filled with respect, love, and happiness.

The process of letting go starts with acknowledging the reality of your situation. It requires a brutally honest assessment of your relationship, devoid of the rose-colored glasses that often cloud judgment. This clarity allows you to see the patterns of behavior that are detrimental to your mental and emotional health. It is about understanding that no amount of effort can change a partner who is unwilling to acknowledge their own toxicity.

Once you have faced this truth, the next step is to reclaim your power. Toxic relationships often strip away your sense of agency, leaving you feeling trapped and helpless. Reclaiming your power involves setting firm boundaries and prioritizing your needs. It means saying no to behaviors that harm you and yes to actions that promote your well-being. It is about rediscovering your voice and using it to advocate for yourself.

Letting go also involves the difficult task of detaching emotionally. This does not mean becoming cold or indifferent, but rather, it is about protecting your heart from further pain. Emotional detachment allows you to view the situation objectively, reducing the emotional hold that your partner may have over you. It empowers you to make decisions based on logic and self-care rather than fear or guilt.

In this process, self-compassion is your greatest ally. It is easy to fall into the trap of self-blame, wondering what you could have done differently to save the marriage. However, it is crucial to remember that the toxicity is not your fault. Treat yourself with the same kindness and understanding that you would offer a dear friend in a similar situation. Celebrate your courage and resilience, and remind yourself that you deserve a life free from pain and suffering.

Support systems play a vital role in letting go. Surround yourself with people who uplift and encourage you, whether they are friends, family, or professional counselors. These individuals can provide the emotional support and practical advice you need to navigate this challenging transition. They can help reinforce your decision and remind you of your worth when doubt creeps in.

Letting go of a toxic marriage is a profound act of self-love. It is about choosing to value yourself enough to walk away from what harms you. It is about believing that you deserve better and having the courage to seek it. By letting go, you open the door to healing, growth, and the possibility of a brighter, healthier future.

Healing From Resentment

Resentment often festers silently, gnawing at the very foundation of our well-being. In the context of a toxic marriage, it can become a formidable barrier to personal happiness and growth. It is imperative to understand that holding onto resentment is akin to drinking poison and expecting the other person to suffer. The only way to truly break free from the chains of a toxic marriage is to heal from this deeply entrenched emotion.

One must first acknowledge the presence of resentment. Denial only prolongs the anguish. By confronting these feelings head-on, you begin the process of liberation. It is not about excusing the behavior that caused the pain but recognizing that clinging to bitterness only harms oneself. Acceptance of these emotions is the first step toward healing.

Next, understanding the root cause of resentment is crucial. Often, it stems from unmet expectations, broken promises, or repeated patterns of disrespect and neglect. By identifying these triggers, you can work towards addressing them effectively. This self-awareness is a powerful tool; it enables you to set boundaries and communicate your needs more clearly, reducing the likelihood of future resentment.

Forgiveness is a potent antidote to resentment. It is not about condoning the actions that hurt you but about releasing the hold they have over your emotional well-being. Forgiving your partner, and crucially, forgiving yourself for any perceived failures, is a transformative act of self-compassion. It allows you to reclaim your power and move forward without the heavy burden of past grievances.

Seeking professional help can be immensely beneficial in this journey. A therapist or counselor can provide a safe space to explore these complex emotions and offer strategies to cope with and overcome them. They can guide you through techniques such as cognitive-behavioral therapy, which can help reframe negative thought patterns and promote a healthier outlook.

Engaging in self-care practices is another essential aspect of healing from resentment. Activities that promote physical and emotional well-being, such as exercise, meditation, and hobbies, can significantly improve your mental state. These practices help in redirecting your focus from the pain to personal growth and fulfillment.

Building a support network is equally important. Surround yourself with friends and family who understand your situation and can offer empathy and encouragement. Sharing your experiences with others who have faced similar challenges can provide comfort and insights on how to navigate this difficult period.

Resentment can cloud your judgment and affect your interactions with others. By working through these emotions, you not only improve your relationship with yourself but also with those around you. It allows you to approach future relationships with a clear mind and an open heart, free from the shadows of past hurts.

Resentment is a heavy chain that binds you to the past. By taking deliberate steps to heal, you can break free and pave the way for a brighter, more fulfilling future. It is a process that requires patience, effort, and a commitment to personal growth, but the rewards are immeasurable. You deserve to live a life unburdened by the weight of resentment, and taking these steps is the key to unlocking that freedom.

Releasing Emotional Baggage

Picture yourself standing at the edge of a vast, serene ocean. The weight of your past burdens feels like a heavy anchor, dragging you down, preventing you from enjoying the tranquility and freedom that lies ahead. This is what emotional baggage from a toxic marriage does to your soul. It holds you back from experiencing the full spectrum of life's possibilities. But imagine the liberation that comes from cutting that anchor loose.

The first step toward this liberation is acknowledging the emotional baggage you carry. Denial only prolongs the suffering. The memories of harsh words, manipulative tactics, and emotional neglect linger like shadows, creeping into every corner of your mind. By confronting these memories head-on, you take the first courageous step towards healing. Acknowledge the pain, the betrayal, the heartache—these emotions are valid and deserve to be recognized.

Forgiveness is often misunderstood as condoning the hurtful actions of others. However, true forgiveness is about freeing yourself from the chains of resentment and anger. Holding onto these negative emotions only poisons your own well-being. Picture forgiveness as a powerful act of self-compassion. By forgiving, you reclaim your power, no longer allowing the toxic actions of another to control your emotional state. This doesn't mean you forget or excuse the behavior; it means you choose peace over perpetual pain.

Self-reflection is another critical component in releasing emotional baggage. Take time to understand your own role in the toxic dynamics. This isn't about blaming yourself but about gaining insights into patterns that you might unconsciously replicate. Were there red flags you ignored? Were there boundaries you failed to set? By understanding these aspects, you equip yourself with the knowledge to avoid similar pitfalls in the future.

Seeking professional help can be incredibly beneficial. Therapists and counselors provide a safe space to explore your emotions and gain perspective. They offer tools and techniques to process trauma and develop healthier coping mechanisms. Don't underestimate the power of professional guidance in navigating these turbulent waters.

Surround yourself with a supportive network. Friends and family who genuinely care about your well-being can offer emotional support and practical advice. Their presence reminds you that you are not alone in this journey. Sharing your experiences with those who understand can be incredibly therapeutic.

Engage in activities that promote emotional healing. Journaling, for instance, allows you to express your feelings freely and reflect on your progress. Physical activities like yoga or hiking can help release pent-up emotions and reduce stress. Creative outlets such as painting or music can also provide a much-needed emotional release.

Mindfulness and meditation practices can help you stay grounded in the present moment. These practices teach you to observe your thoughts and feelings without judgment, reducing the emotional grip of past traumas. As you cultivate mindfulness, you'll find that the emotional baggage begins to lose its weight, allowing you to experience life more fully and joyfully.

Reclaiming your emotional freedom is an empowering process. It's about taking control of your narrative and deciding that your past will not dictate your future. By releasing the emotional baggage of a toxic marriage, you open the door to new beginnings, healthier relationships, and a more fulfilling life. Imagine the lightness of being unburdened, the joy of living authentically, and the strength of a spirit that has overcome adversity. This is the transformative power of letting go.

Finding Peace

Breaking free from a toxic marriage is undeniably one of the most challenging yet liberating decisions one can make. The emotional turmoil, self-doubt, and fear of the unknown can create an overwhelming sense of paralysis. However, it is crucial to recognize that peace is not a distant dream but a tangible reality waiting to be grasped. The first step toward this newfound tranquility begins with the acknowledgment that you deserve better.

Imagine waking up each morning without the weight of constant criticism or the anxiety of impending conflict. Picture a life where your thoughts and feelings are valued, where you can express yourself freely without fear of retribution. This is not a fantasy; it is a viable future that starts with the courage to prioritize your well-being.

The decision to leave a toxic relationship is often clouded by a sense of guilt or obligation. Society, family, and even our own minds can create a narrative that staying is a testament to commitment and strength. But true strength lies in recognizing when a situation is detrimental to your mental and emotional health. It takes immense courage to walk away from something familiar, even if it is harmful, and to step into the unknown. Yet, it is in this unknown that you will find the opportunity for growth and healing.

Consider the long-term impact of remaining in a toxic marriage. The continuous exposure to negativity can erode your self-esteem and lead to chronic stress, anxiety, and even depression. Your physical health can also suffer, manifesting in ailments that stem from prolonged emotional distress. By choosing to stay, you are inadvertently allowing the toxicity to take root deeper within you, making it harder to extricate yourself later.

On the other hand, choosing to leave opens the door to rediscovering yourself. It allows you to reconnect with your passions, interests, and the aspects of your personality that may have been suppressed. This journey of self-discovery is not just about healing but about thriving. It is about reclaiming your life and living it on your own terms.

Support systems play a crucial role in this transition. Surround yourself with friends, family, and professionals who understand your situation and can offer both emotional and practical support. Therapy and support groups can provide a safe space to process your feelings and develop coping strategies. Remember, asking for help is not a sign of weakness but a step toward empowerment.

Financial independence is another critical factor. Ensuring that you have the means to support yourself can alleviate some of the fear associated with leaving. This might involve seeking legal advice, understanding your rights, and planning your finances meticulously. The more prepared you are, the smoother the transition will be.

Visualize the life you aspire to lead. A life where your home is a sanctuary, filled with positivity and free from the shadows of conflict. A life where you can pursue your dreams without the constant drag of negativity. This vision is not just possible; it is within your reach. The path to finding peace begins with the decision to value yourself enough to walk away from toxicity. It is a journey worth taking, for the peace that awaits on the other side is immeasurable.

Chapter 10:
Reclaim Your Life

Taking Control

Breaking free from a toxic marriage is not just about leaving; it's about reclaiming your life, your self-worth, and your future. The first step towards liberation is understanding that you have the power to take control. Often, individuals trapped in toxic relationships feel powerless, as if their identity and choices are dictated by their partner. This perception is fostered by manipulation, emotional abuse, and constant belittlement, but it is not the reality. The truth is, the power to change your life lies within you.

Recognizing the signs of a toxic marriage is paramount. Emotional abuse, manipulation, and a consistent feeling of being undervalued are red flags that shouldn't be ignored. These signs are often subtle, making it easy to dismiss them as normal marital issues. However, the persistent nature of these behaviors can erode your self-esteem and sense of self. Acknowledging that these patterns are harmful is the first step towards taking control.

Taking control means setting boundaries. Boundaries are essential for your mental and emotional health. They define what you will and will not tolerate in any relationship. In a toxic marriage, establishing boundaries can be challenging, especially if your partner is used to having control. Nevertheless, it is crucial to assert your needs and protect your well-being. This might mean limiting interactions, refusing to engage in arguments, or seeking support from trusted friends and family.

Empowerment comes through knowledge. Educating yourself about toxic relationships and understanding the dynamics at play can provide clarity and strength. Knowledge is a powerful tool that can help you see your situation from a new perspective. Books, support groups, and professional counseling can offer insights and strategies to cope with and eventually leave a toxic marriage. Remember, seeking help is not a sign of weakness but a step towards regaining control of your life.

Financial independence is another critical aspect of taking control. Many individuals stay in toxic marriages due to financial dependence on their partner. Assess your financial situation and explore ways to become self-sufficient. This might involve seeking employment, furthering your education, or consulting a financial advisor. Financial independence can provide the freedom and security needed to leave a toxic relationship and start anew.

Building a support network is vital. Surround yourself with people who uplift and encourage you. Isolation is a common tactic in toxic relationships, as it makes you more dependent on your partner. Reconnecting with friends and family can provide emotional support and practical assistance. Don't hesitate to reach out to support groups or professional counselors who specialize in helping individuals in toxic relationships.

Taking control also involves envisioning a future free from toxicity. Visualize what a healthy, fulfilling life looks like for you. Set goals and make plans for your future. This vision can serve as a powerful motivator, reminding you why taking control is essential. It's about creating a life where you are valued, respected, and happy.

The journey towards freedom from a toxic marriage is undoubtedly challenging, but the first and most crucial step is to take control. By recognizing the signs, setting boundaries, empowering yourself with knowledge, achieving financial independence, building a support network, and envisioning a brighter future, you can break the chains of a toxic marriage and reclaim your life. The power is within you.

Creating a Vision for Your Life

Imagine waking up each morning with a sense of purpose, clarity, and direction. Picture a life where you feel empowered, joyous, and free from the emotional shackles that have held you back for so long. This is not a distant dream but a reality waiting to be crafted by you. The first step towards this transformation is creating a vision for your life, a roadmap that will guide you through the tumultuous journey of breaking free from a toxic marriage.

A vision for your life is not just a collection of random wishes or fleeting desires. It is a detailed, vivid picture of the future you want to build. It is the North Star that will keep you focused and motivated, even when the road gets rough. Without a clear vision, it is easy to get lost in the maze of emotions, doubts, and setbacks that come with ending a toxic relationship.

To start, take a moment to reflect on what truly matters to you. What are your core values? What brings you joy and fulfillment? This introspection is crucial because your vision should be aligned with your authentic self, not a version of you shaped by the toxic dynamics of your marriage. Write down your thoughts, dreams, and aspirations. Be as specific as possible. The more detailed your vision, the more tangible and achievable it becomes.

Next, consider the different aspects of your life that you want to transform. Your vision should encompass your emotional well-being, career, relationships, health, and personal growth. For instance, you might envision a life where you have a career that excites you, friendships that uplift you, and a sense of inner peace that comes from self-acceptance and love. Visualize yourself thriving in these areas, free from the negativity and constraints of your current situation.

Creating a vision is not just about dreaming big; it's also about setting realistic and actionable goals. Break down your vision into smaller, manageable steps. What can you do today, this week, or this month to move closer to your ideal life? These steps might include seeking therapy, joining a support group, updating your resume, or simply practicing self-care. Each small victory will build momentum, reinforcing your belief that a better life is within reach.

It is also essential to anticipate and prepare for obstacles. Ending a toxic marriage is a complex and emotionally charged process. There will be moments of doubt, fear, and even regret. Having a clear vision will help you stay resilient during these challenging times. Remind yourself why you are making these changes and how they align with your long-term happiness and well-being.

Share your vision with trusted friends, family, or a mentor. Their support and encouragement can provide you with the strength and motivation you need to stay on track. Surrounding yourself with positive influences will help you maintain a hopeful outlook and keep you accountable to your goals.

In the process of creating a vision for your life, you are not just planning for the future; you are reclaiming your power and autonomy. You are taking control of your destiny and refusing to let the toxicity of your marriage define you. This vision is your beacon of hope, your guiding light, and your promise to yourself that you deserve a life filled with love, respect, and happiness.

Setting Goals and Taking Action

Imagine a life where you wake up every morning with a sense of purpose, free from the suffocating constraints of a toxic marriage. This is not a distant dream; it is a reality within your reach. The first step to transforming your life is setting clear, achievable goals and taking decisive action.

Why are goals so crucial? Because they serve as your roadmap out of the labyrinth of toxicity. Without goals, you are like a ship adrift at sea, vulnerable to the whims of the storm. By setting specific, measurable, attainable, relevant, and time-bound (SMART) goals, you give yourself direction and momentum. These goals become your guiding stars, leading you toward a healthier, happier existence.

Start by identifying what you truly want. Take a moment to visualize your ideal life. What does it look like? What does it feel like? Write these visions down. This exercise is not just about wishful thinking; it is about creating a tangible, actionable plan. When you put your dreams on paper, they transform from abstract thoughts into concrete objectives.

Next, break these objectives into manageable steps. A goal without a plan is merely a wish. For example, if your goal is to regain financial independence, start by creating a budget, seeking employment, or consulting a financial advisor. If your goal is to rebuild your self-esteem, consider therapy, joining support groups, or engaging in activities that make you feel good about yourself. Each small step you take builds momentum, gradually leading you toward your larger goal.

Taking action can be daunting, especially when you are trapped in a toxic environment. Fear and doubt may cloud your judgment, making you question your decisions. But remember, every journey begins with a single step. The key is to start, no matter how small the action may seem. Progress, however incremental, is still progress.

Accountability plays a pivotal role in achieving your goals. Share your aspirations with trusted friends or family members who can offer support and encouragement. Their belief in you can bolster your confidence and keep you motivated. Additionally, consider seeking professional guidance from a therapist or life coach. These experts can provide valuable insights and strategies tailored to your unique situation.

Do not underestimate the power of self-compassion. Leaving a toxic marriage is a monumental task, and setbacks are inevitable. Instead of berating yourself for perceived failures, acknowledge your efforts and celebrate your victories, no matter how minor they may appear. Every step forward is a testament to your strength and resilience.

Remember, you have the power to change your life. Setting goals and taking action are not just tools—they are your lifeline to freedom and fulfillment. The path may be challenging, but the reward is a life unshackled from the chains of toxicity. Believe in yourself and take that first step today. Your future self will thank you.

Living Authentically

A life lived authentically is a life lived with purpose and clarity. In the context of escaping the chains of a toxic marriage, authenticity becomes not just a choice, but a necessity. It's about shedding the layers of pretense and expectation that have been imposed upon you, and rediscovering the person you truly are. This journey towards authenticity is not merely self-serving; it is an act of reclamation, a powerful statement that you refuse to be defined by the toxicity of your past.

Consider the weight that is lifted when you no longer have to maintain a facade. Toxic relationships often demand that you suppress your true self to cater to another's needs, whims, or manipulations. Living authentically means rejecting this suppression and asserting your right to be seen and heard as you genuinely are. It means acknowledging your own needs, desires, and values, and acting in accordance with them. This is not an easy task, but it is a profoundly liberating one.

Living authentically requires courage. It necessitates that you confront the fears and insecurities that have kept you tethered to a toxic relationship. These fears might include the fear of being alone, the fear of judgment, or the fear of failure. However, by facing these fears head-on, you dismantle their power over you. You begin to realize that the strength to live authentically comes from within, not from external validation or approval.

Moreover, authenticity fosters genuine connections. When you present yourself as you truly are, you attract people who appreciate and value the real you. This is in stark contrast to the superficial connections that often characterize toxic relationships, where interactions are based on manipulation and control rather than mutual respect and understanding. By being authentic, you create the possibility for deeper, more meaningful relationships that are based on trust and honesty.

Authenticity also means taking responsibility for your own happiness. It's about recognizing that you are the author of your own story. In a toxic marriage, it's easy to fall into the trap of blaming your partner for your unhappiness. While it's true that their behavior may have contributed to your distress, living authentically means acknowledging that you have the power to change your circumstances. You have the agency to make decisions that align with your true self and lead to a more fulfilling life.

The path to authenticity is not without its challenges. It requires ongoing self-reflection and a willingness to make difficult choices. It might mean distancing yourself from people or situations that no longer serve your well-being. It might involve seeking support from friends, family, or professionals who can help you navigate this transformative process. But every step taken towards authenticity is a step towards freedom.

In the end, living authentically is about reclaiming your life and your identity. It's about breaking free from the chains of a toxic marriage and stepping into a future where you are true to yourself. This authenticity becomes the foundation upon which you build a life of purpose, joy, and genuine connection. It is a powerful antidote to the toxicity that once held you captive, and it is the key to unlocking a life of true fulfillment.

Embracing Your Future

Breaking free from a toxic marriage is not merely about severing ties with a past that no longer serves you; it is about stepping into a future that holds endless possibilities. It's time to envision a life where your happiness, growth, and well-being are the priorities. The path forward may seem daunting, but it's filled with opportunities for renewal and self-discovery.

Picture yourself waking up every morning with a sense of peace and excitement about the day ahead. This is not a distant dream but a tangible reality waiting for you. By letting go of the toxic relationship, you are making space for positive experiences and healthy connections. Imagine the relief of no longer walking on eggshells, the joy of pursuing your passions without fear of criticism, and the freedom to express your true self.

The first step towards this brighter future is to establish a vision for what you want your life to look like. Take a moment to reflect on your dreams, aspirations, and values. What activities bring you joy? What kind of people do you want to surround yourself with? What goals have you set aside that you are now ready to pursue? Write these down and keep them in a place where you can revisit them regularly. This vision will serve as your guiding light, keeping you focused and motivated.

Next, consider the practical steps needed to achieve this vision. This might include seeking therapy to process your experiences and heal from the trauma, building a support network of friends and family, or even pursuing educational or career opportunities that you had previously put on hold. Each small step you take is a victory, moving you closer to the life you deserve.

It's also crucial to cultivate a mindset of resilience and self-compassion. You may encounter setbacks and moments of self-doubt, but these are merely temporary obstacles. Remind yourself of your strength and the progress you have already made. Celebrate your achievements, no matter how small they may seem. You have already taken the courageous step of leaving a toxic marriage; you are capable of much more than you realize.

Surround yourself with positivity. Engage in activities that uplift your spirit and contribute to your sense of well-being. This could be anything from practicing mindfulness and meditation to engaging in hobbies that bring you joy. Connecting with others who have gone through similar experiences can also provide invaluable support and encouragement.

Financial independence is another key aspect of securing your future. Take control of your finances by creating a budget, saving for the future, and seeking advice from financial experts if necessary. Financial stability will not only provide peace of mind but also empower you to make decisions that align with your best interests.

As you move forward, remember that your future is a blank canvas, ready to be painted with the vibrant colors of your choosing. The pain of the past does not define you; it has equipped you with the strength and wisdom to create a fulfilling and joyful life. Allow yourself to dream big, to take risks, and to embrace the opportunities that come your way. Your future is bright, and it is yours to shape.

Chapter 11:
Moving Forward: Building Healthy Relationships

Understanding Healthy Relationships

A life free from the suffocating grip of a toxic marriage is not only possible but absolutely essential for your well-being. The first step towards this liberation is recognizing and understanding what a healthy relationship looks like. It's crucial to grasp that a healthy relationship serves as a foundation for personal happiness, emotional stability, and overall life satisfaction. Unlike the constant turmoil of a toxic marriage, a healthy relationship is built on mutual respect, trust, and genuine affection.

Imagine waking up each day feeling valued, loved, and supported by a partner who truly cares about your well-being. This isn't a mere fantasy; it's the hallmark of a healthy relationship. In such a partnership, both individuals feel free to express their thoughts and emotions without fear of judgment or reprisal. Communication flows effortlessly, paving the way for deeper understanding and connection. This starkly contrasts with the walking-on-eggshells atmosphere typical of toxic marriages, where every word and action is scrutinized and often criticized.

Trust is another cornerstone of a healthy relationship. In a nurturing partnership, trust isn't just given; it's earned and continuously nurtured. Both partners feel secure knowing they can rely on each other, whether it's for emotional support, financial stability, or simply being there during tough times. This level of trust fosters a sense of safety and security, allowing both individuals to grow and thrive. Compare this to a toxic marriage, where mistrust and suspicion erode the very fabric of the relationship, leaving both parties in a constant state of anxiety and doubt.

Respect is equally vital. In a healthy relationship, both partners honor each other's individuality, dreams, and aspirations. They celebrate each other's successes and offer unwavering support during failures. This mutual respect creates an environment where both individuals feel empowered to pursue their goals and become the best versions of themselves. Contrast this with a toxic marriage, where one partner often undermines the other's self-worth, dreams, and accomplishments, trapping them in a cycle of dependency and despair.

Healthy relationships also thrive on equality and partnership. Decisions are made together, responsibilities are shared, and both partners contribute to the relationship's overall well-being. This sense of equality fosters a balanced and harmonious life, where both individuals feel valued and appreciated. In a toxic marriage, however, power imbalances are rampant. One partner often dominates, making unilateral decisions and imposing their will, leaving the other feeling powerless and marginalized.

Emotional support is the glue that holds a healthy relationship together. In a nurturing partnership, both individuals are attuned to each other's emotional needs. They offer comfort, encouragement, and a listening ear, especially during challenging times. This emotional support fosters a deep sense of connection and intimacy, making life's inevitable ups and downs more manageable. In stark contrast, a toxic marriage often lacks this emotional support. Instead of offering comfort and understanding, one partner may belittle, criticize, or emotionally withdraw, leaving the other feeling isolated and unsupported.

Understanding these fundamental aspects of a healthy relationship is the first step towards breaking free from the chains of a toxic marriage. Recognizing what you deserve and what is possible can empower you to make the necessary changes for a happier, healthier future.

Qualities of a Healthy Relationship

A key to breaking free from the chains of a toxic marriage lies not just in recognizing the harmful patterns but also in understanding what a healthy relationship looks like. To rebuild your life and open your heart to future possibilities, it's crucial to grasp the qualities that define a nurturing and supportive partnership. Imagine a relationship where mutual respect, trust, and love form the foundation. This is not a far-fetched dream but an attainable reality that you deserve.

In a healthy relationship, mutual respect stands paramount. This means valuing each other's opinions, feelings, and boundaries. When respect is present, disagreements don't escalate into hurtful arguments. Instead, they become opportunities for growth and understanding. Picture yourself in a relationship where your voice is heard and your feelings are validated. This is a stark contrast to the dismissiveness and belittlement often found in toxic marriages. Mutual respect fosters an environment where both partners feel valued and important.

Trust is another cornerstone of a healthy relationship. Without trust, a relationship is built on shaky ground. Trust means being able to rely on your partner, knowing that they have your best interests at heart. It's about feeling secure in the relationship, confident that your partner is honest and faithful. This sense of security is often missing in toxic marriages, where deceit and betrayal can erode the foundation of the relationship. Envision a relationship where you can share your deepest secrets without fear of judgment or betrayal, where trust is not a luxury but a given.

Communication in a healthy relationship is open, honest, and respectful. Effective communication involves not just speaking but also listening. It's about expressing your needs and concerns without fear of retribution. In a toxic marriage, communication is often one-sided or manipulative, leading to misunderstandings and resentment. Imagine a relationship where you can discuss your feelings openly, where conflicts are resolved through dialogue and compromise rather than through shouting matches or silent treatments. This level of communication is essential for emotional intimacy and connection.

Emotional support is another vital quality. In a healthy relationship, partners are each other's biggest cheerleaders. They provide comfort and encouragement during tough times and celebrate each other's successes. This support system is often absent in toxic marriages, where one partner may feel isolated and unsupported. Visualize a relationship where your partner is your rock, someone who stands by you through thick and thin, offering a shoulder to lean on and a hand to hold.

Equality is also a hallmark of a healthy relationship. Both partners share responsibilities and decision-making equally. There is no power struggle or dominance, but rather a balanced partnership where both individuals contribute to the relationship's success. In contrast, toxic marriages often feature power imbalances, with one partner exerting control over the other. Imagine a relationship where decisions are made together, where both partners feel empowered and respected.

Finally, a healthy relationship is characterized by love and affection. This is not just about physical intimacy but also about emotional closeness and a deep bond. Love in a healthy relationship is unconditional and nurturing, providing a safe haven from the stresses of the outside world. In toxic marriages, love is often conditional, used as a tool for manipulation. Picture a relationship where love is freely given and received, where you feel cherished and appreciated every single day.

Understanding these qualities is not just theoretical; it's a practical guide to what you should seek in your relationships. You deserve a partnership that lifts you up, supports you, and makes you feel truly loved. Don't settle for anything less.

Navigating New Relationships

Leaving a toxic marriage is a monumental step towards reclaiming your life and self-worth. Yet, this newfound freedom often brings the challenge of building new relationships. It's easy to carry the scars of your past into new connections, but doing so can hinder your ability to truly heal and grow. You deserve relationships that nurture your well-being, encourage your growth, and celebrate your individuality.

First and foremost, understanding your own worth is crucial. Toxic relationships often erode self-esteem, leaving you questioning your value. Take this time to rediscover your strengths, passions, and aspirations. Engage in activities that make you feel alive and confident. The more you invest in yourself, the clearer your boundaries and expectations will become. This clarity is vital for attracting healthy relationships where mutual respect and admiration are foundational.

Next, be mindful of the patterns that previously led you into a toxic relationship. Reflect on the red flags you may have ignored or rationalized. Trust your intuition and be vigilant about recognizing similar warning signs in new acquaintances. Establishing boundaries early on is not only a form of self-protection but also a way to communicate your needs and values to potential partners. Healthy individuals will respect these boundaries, while those who don't are likely not worth your time and energy.

Building a support system of friends and family who genuinely care for you can provide a safety net as you navigate new relationships. Share your experiences and feelings with those who have your best interests at heart. Their insights can offer valuable perspectives and help you stay grounded. Having a strong support system also means you're less likely to fall back into unhealthy patterns out of loneliness or desperation.

While it's natural to feel a sense of urgency to fill the void left by your previous relationship, rushing into new connections can be detrimental. Take the time to get to know someone before fully committing. Look for qualities that align with your values and long-term goals. Patience allows you to build a relationship based on genuine compatibility rather than a fleeting sense of relief from loneliness.

The void left by a past relationship might drive one to seek comfort and companionship quickly, but rushing into new connections often results in poor choices and may lead to further heartache. One should look for qualities that align with one's values and long-term goals, by cultivating meaningful relationships based on compatibility and shared vision, rather than immediate emotional relief.

Before seeking a new relationship, it's essential to reflect on what went wrong in the previous one. Understand your emotional needs, desires, and what you want from future relationships.

Don't rush into forming a new bond. Developing meaningful connections takes time. Patience allows for a deeper understanding of the person you are engaging with, ensuring you're not just filling a temporary void.

Look for people who share your core values. Relationships rooted in shared beliefs and principles are more likely to thrive. Whether it's honesty, kindness, ambition, or spirituality, these core elements are foundational for long-term compatibility.

While chemistry may create an initial spark, lasting relationships are built on character. Observe how the person treats others, responds to challenges, and handles conflicts. These indicators reveal much about a person's long-term suitability as a partner or friend.

Seek relationships that encourage personal growth. Whether it's a life partner or friend, the relationship should inspire mutual development. A true connection fosters an environment of support, learning, and evolution.

Establishing boundaries early on creates a healthy dynamic and ensures that both individuals are respected. Relationships built on mutual respect and clear boundaries have a solid foundation.

In forming new relationships, the key is to be thoughtful and deliberate. Rushed connections often lead to repeating past mistakes, while slow, intentional choices allow for a lasting partnership or friendship that can withstand time and challenges.

Communication is another cornerstone of healthy relationships. Be open about your past and the lessons you've learned, but also be willing to listen and understand your partner's experiences and viewpoints. Effective communication fosters trust and intimacy, creating a solid foundation for a lasting relationship. It's essential to cultivate an environment where both partners feel heard and valued.

Lastly, don't underestimate the importance of professional guidance. Therapists and counselors can offer invaluable tools and strategies for navigating new relationships. They can help you process lingering trauma and build the emotional resilience needed for a healthy partnership. Investing in your mental health is a powerful step towards ensuring that your next relationship is built on a foundation of mutual respect, love, and understanding.

Navigating new relationships after escaping a toxic marriage is undoubtedly challenging, but it is also an opportunity for profound growth and transformation. By valuing yourself, recognizing unhealthy patterns, building a supportive network, exercising patience, communicating effectively, and seeking professional help, you set the stage for relationships that enrich your life rather than diminish it. You have the power to create connections that reflect the strength and resilience you've cultivated through your journey.

Setting and Maintaining Boundaries

Imagine a life where your needs are respected, your emotions validated, and your personal space honored. This is not a distant fantasy but an achievable reality, especially when you learn to set and maintain boundaries effectively. Boundaries are not walls to keep others out but bridges to healthier relationships and self-respect. They are essential in escaping the chains of a toxic marriage, ensuring that you reclaim your autonomy and inner peace.

In toxic relationships, boundaries are often blurred or completely disregarded. This lack of respect for personal limits can lead to a cycle of emotional and psychological abuse, where one partner dominates and the other is left feeling powerless and insignificant. Establishing boundaries is an act of self-love and empowerment. It is the first step towards breaking free from the oppressive grip of a toxic marriage.

Begin by identifying your limits. Reflect on what behaviors and situations make you uncomfortable, anxious, or disrespected. These feelings are indicators that your boundaries are being violated. Write them down and be specific. This clarity will serve as your guide in communicating your needs assertively.

Communication is key to boundary-setting. Approach the conversation with honesty and calmness. Use "I" statements to express how certain actions affect you and what changes you need. For instance, instead of saying, "You never listen to me," try, "I feel unheard when my opinions are dismissed, and I need us to have more open and respectful conversations." This approach reduces defensiveness and focuses on your feelings and needs.

Consistency is crucial in maintaining boundaries. Once established, enforce them firmly yet respectfully. Toxic partners may test your limits, hoping you'll revert to old patterns. Stand your ground. Reiterate your boundaries and the consequences of violating them. This might feel uncomfortable initially, but remember, each time you uphold your boundaries, you are reinforcing your worth and paving the way for a healthier dynamic.

Self-care is a vital component of this process. Prioritize activities that nourish your mind, body, and soul. Surround yourself with supportive friends and family who respect your boundaries. Engage in hobbies and practices that bring you joy and relaxation. This not only strengthens your resolve but also reminds you of the life and happiness you deserve.

Educate yourself about healthy relationships and boundaries. Seek resources such as books, workshops, or therapy. Understanding the principles of mutual respect and communication will empower you to recognize and demand the same in your marriage.

Remember, setting boundaries is not about changing your partner but about protecting yourself. It is about creating a safe space where you can thrive emotionally and mentally. If your partner is unwilling to respect your boundaries despite your efforts, it may be a sign that the relationship is irreparably toxic. In such cases, seeking professional guidance or considering separation might be necessary for your well-being.

Your happiness and peace are worth fighting for. By setting and maintaining boundaries, you are taking a bold step towards a life free from the chains of toxicity. You are reclaiming your power, honoring your self-worth, and opening the door to a future filled with respect, love, and genuine connection.

Communicating Effectively

In the labyrinth of a toxic marriage, communication often becomes the first casualty, and yet it holds the key to any hope of resolution and healing. Effective communication isn't merely about exchanging words; it's about fostering understanding, trust, and respect. Imagine a bridge, sturdy and reliable, that connects two islands. Without it, each island remains isolated, unable to share resources or understand the conditions on the other side. This bridge is your lifeline, your means to navigate the tumultuous waters of a strained relationship.

Consider the impact of choosing words with intention. In a toxic marriage, words can be weapons or tools of healing. The tone, context, and timing of your conversations play pivotal roles. It's essential to express feelings without assigning blame. Instead of saying, "You never listen to me," try, "I feel unheard when we talk." This subtle shift transforms an accusation into an expression of your emotional state, paving the way for empathy rather than defensiveness.

Listening, truly listening, is equally important. It requires more than just hearing the words; it involves understanding the emotions and intentions behind them. Active listening means giving your partner your undivided attention, acknowledging their perspective without immediately formulating a response. This practice not only validates their feelings but also opens a path to mutual respect and understanding.

Non-verbal communication often speaks louder than words. Body language, facial expressions, and even silence convey messages that can either bridge gaps or widen them. Maintaining eye contact, nodding in agreement, or offering a comforting touch can reinforce verbal communication, showing that you are engaged and empathetic. Conversely, crossed arms, rolling eyes, or turning away can communicate disinterest or disdain, exacerbating the toxicity.

Conflict is inevitable, but how you handle it can make a significant difference. Approach disagreements with a mindset geared towards resolution rather than victory. This means prioritizing the relationship over being right. It's about finding common ground and compromising where necessary. Employing "I" statements rather than "you" statements can help keep the focus on your feelings and experiences rather than placing blame on your partner.

Establishing boundaries is another cornerstone of effective communication. Boundaries define what is acceptable and what isn't, creating a safe space for both partners. They are not walls to keep your partner out but guidelines that foster respect and understanding. Clear, consistent boundaries help prevent misunderstandings and ensure that both parties feel valued and respected.

Empathy is the glue that binds effective communication. Putting yourself in your partner's shoes, trying to understand their emotions and perspectives, can transform the dynamic of your interactions. Empathy fosters compassion and reduces the impulse to react defensively or dismissively. It builds a foundation of mutual respect and understanding, essential for navigating the complexities of a toxic marriage.

Effective communication is not a magic cure, but it is a powerful tool. It requires patience, practice, and a willingness to be vulnerable. The effort you invest in communicating effectively can create ripples of change, gradually transforming the toxic environment into one where understanding and respect can flourish. This bridge of communication can support you in your journey towards healing, whether it leads to reconciliation or a healthier separation.

Chapter 12:
Empowering Yourself

Building Resilience

Every person deserves a life filled with love, respect, and mutual support. Yet, many find themselves trapped in toxic marriages, where emotional, verbal, or even physical abuse becomes a daily ordeal. The chains of such relationships can be incredibly difficult to break, but building resilience is the key to reclaiming your life and securing a brighter, healthier future.

Resilience is not an innate trait that you either possess or lack; it is a skill that can be developed and strengthened over time. The first step in cultivating resilience is acknowledging that you have the power to change your circumstances. Many people in toxic marriages feel powerless, believing that their situation is unchangeable. However, accepting that you have the agency to make different choices is the foundation upon which resilience is built.

Self-awareness is another crucial element. Begin by recognizing the patterns of behavior that have kept you ensnared in the toxic cycle. Are you constantly making excuses for your partner's behavior? Do you find yourself isolating from friends and family to avoid embarrassment or judgment? Identifying these patterns is the initial step toward breaking them. Write down your thoughts and feelings; seeing them in black and white can provide a new level of clarity and motivate you to take action.

Support systems play a pivotal role in building resilience. Surrounding yourself with people who uplift and encourage you can make a world of difference. Confide in trusted friends or family members who can provide emotional support and practical advice. Professional help, such as therapy or counseling, can offer an impartial perspective and equip you with coping mechanisms to deal with the challenges ahead.

It is also important to set realistic, achievable goals. Leaving a toxic marriage is not an overnight process; it requires careful planning and execution. Start small. Perhaps your first goal is to set aside a little money each month to build a financial cushion. Maybe it's about finding a support group or attending counseling sessions. Each small victory builds momentum, reinforcing your resilience and preparing you for larger, more significant steps.

Self-care cannot be overstated. A toxic marriage can severely impact your mental and physical health. Prioritize activities that rejuvenate your spirit and body. Exercise, meditation, and hobbies you enjoy can serve as vital outlets for stress and anxiety. When you take care of your well-being, you are better equipped to handle the emotional and physical toll of leaving a toxic relationship.

Educating yourself is another powerful tool. Knowledge is empowering, and understanding the dynamics of toxic relationships can provide you with the insight needed to navigate your situation effectively. Read books, attend workshops, or join online forums where you can learn from others who have successfully escaped similar circumstances.

Building resilience is an ongoing process, requiring patience and persistent effort. Each step you take, no matter how small, brings you closer to a life free from the chains of a toxic marriage. Remember, the path to freedom and happiness is within your reach. By cultivating resilience, you not only survive but thrive, transforming your life into one filled with hope, joy, and endless possibilities.

Self-Empowerment Techniques

In the tumultuous landscape of a toxic marriage, finding your own strength can feel like an insurmountable challenge. Yet, it is precisely in these moments of despair that the seeds of self-empowerment must be sown. Imagine the liberation that comes when you reclaim control over your life, your emotions, and your future. This transformation is not just a possibility; it is a necessity. It begins with a commitment to yourself, to rise above the toxicity and rediscover the person you were always meant to be.

One of the most powerful tools at your disposal is the practice of setting boundaries. Boundaries are not walls to keep others out, but rather, they are gates that allow you to protect your well-being. They are vital in a toxic marriage, where your emotional and physical space can easily be encroached upon. Start by identifying what behaviors you will no longer tolerate. Communicate these limits clearly and firmly. Remember, you have the right to demand respect and consideration. This act of self-assertion is the first step toward reclaiming your autonomy.

Another critical technique is cultivating a support system. Isolation is a common weapon in the arsenal of a toxic partner, designed to make you feel alone and powerless. Break free from this isolation by reaching out to friends, family, or support groups. Surround yourself with people who uplift and encourage you. Their perspectives can offer valuable insights and their support can fortify your resolve. It is in the company of these allies that you will find the strength to stand tall and move forward.

Equally important is the practice of self-care. In the chaos of a toxic marriage, self-care often falls by the wayside. Reclaim it with vigor. Engage in activities that nourish your body, mind, and soul. Whether it's a quiet walk in nature, a hobby you love, or simply taking time to rest, these moments of self-care are acts of defiance against the toxicity that seeks to consume you. They are declarations of your worth and a reminder that you deserve joy and peace.

Empowerment also comes through self-reflection. Take time to understand your emotions, your triggers, and your responses. Journaling can be an invaluable tool in this process. It allows you to process your thoughts and feelings, providing clarity and insight. Reflect on your strengths and achievements, no matter how small they may seem. Celebrate these victories as they are testament to your resilience and capacity for growth.

Lastly, educate yourself. Knowledge is a formidable ally in the battle against toxicity. Learn about the dynamics of toxic relationships, understand the tactics of manipulation and control, and arm yourself with strategies to counter them. This awareness not only equips you with practical tools but also demystifies the behavior of your toxic partner, reducing their power over you.

Each of these techniques is a step toward reclaiming your power and rebuilding your life. They are not mere suggestions; they are lifelines. By implementing them, you are not only escaping the chains of a toxic marriage but also forging a path to a future defined by strength, dignity, and self-respect. You owe it to yourself to seize these tools and transform your life. The power to change is within you, and now is the time to unleash it.

Developing Emotional Intelligence

Emotional intelligence is the compass that will guide you through the stormy seas of a toxic marriage and lead you to calmer waters. It's not just a buzzword; it's a vital skill that can transform your life and empower you to make healthier decisions. Imagine being able to understand and manage your emotions, as well as those of your partner, with clarity and confidence. This capability can be the key to breaking free from the chains of a toxic relationship.

Start by acknowledging your feelings, no matter how messy or overwhelming they might seem. Denial only prolongs the suffering, but acceptance is the first step toward healing. Consider keeping a journal where you can freely express your thoughts and emotions. Writing them down can be incredibly liberating and offers a safe space to confront your reality. This practice can help you identify patterns in your behavior and emotional responses, providing valuable insights into your emotional landscape.

Next, cultivate empathy, but not just for your partner—extend it to yourself. Self-compassion is crucial when dealing with the fallout of a toxic marriage. You might have internalized blame or guilt, but it's important to recognize that you deserve kindness and understanding. Treat yourself as you would a dear friend who is going through a tough time. This shift in perspective can reduce self-criticism and build emotional resilience.

Active listening is another cornerstone of emotional intelligence. In the chaos of a toxic marriage, communication often breaks down, turning into a series of accusations and defenses. By practicing active listening, you can defuse some of the tension and create a space for more constructive dialogue. This doesn't mean you have to agree with everything your partner says, but it does mean giving them the courtesy of being heard. This simple act can sometimes reveal underlying issues that need addressing, rather than just the surface-level conflicts.

Setting boundaries is an act of emotional intelligence that cannot be overstated. Boundaries are not about building walls but about creating healthy limits that protect your well-being. Clearly communicate what is acceptable and what is not. This might be challenging initially, especially if you are accustomed to a dynamic where boundaries are frequently crossed. However, maintaining these limits is essential for your emotional health and can prevent further damage.

Mindfulness and emotional regulation are skills that can be honed through practice. Mindfulness involves staying present and fully engaging with the moment, which can help you manage stress and reduce anxiety. Techniques such as deep breathing, meditation, or even mindful walking can ground you when emotions run high. Emotional regulation, on the other hand, is about managing your reactions to those emotions. It's not about suppressing them but rather finding healthy outlets for expression.

Lastly, seek support. Emotional intelligence also involves recognizing when you need help and being willing to ask for it. Whether it's through therapy, support groups, or trusted friends and family, surrounding yourself with a network of support can make a significant difference. These resources can provide perspectives and coping strategies that you might not have considered, further aiding your emotional growth.

Developing emotional intelligence is not a quick fix but a lifelong journey. However, the rewards are immense. It equips you with the tools to navigate not just the complexities of a toxic marriage but also the broader challenges of life. By investing in your emotional intelligence, you are investing in a healthier, more fulfilling future.

Harnessing Your Strengths

In the midst of a toxic marriage, it is easy to forget that you possess immense strength and resilience. These are not just abstract qualities but tangible assets that can be harnessed to change your life. Recognizing and utilizing your strengths is not just an option; it is a necessity for breaking free from the chains that bind you.

Consider the emotional fortitude you have demonstrated thus far. Surviving in a toxic environment requires a level of mental toughness that many people never have to develop. This mental toughness is a powerful tool. It means you have the capacity to endure hardship and still keep moving forward. Imagine what you could achieve if you directed this strength towards building a new, healthier life for yourself.

Your intuition is another invaluable asset. Over time, you have likely developed a keen sense of awareness about your partner's moods, intentions, and actions. This heightened intuition can be redirected to protect yourself and make wise decisions. Trusting your gut feelings can guide you towards safer environments and healthier relationships.

Your problem-solving abilities have also been honed to perfection. In a toxic marriage, you have had to navigate countless obstacles and crises. This experience has equipped you with the skills to think on your feet and devise solutions under pressure. These problem-solving skills are not limited to your current predicament; they are transferable to any challenge you might face in the future.

Additionally, consider your support network, however small it might be. Whether it's a close friend, a family member, or a support group, these connections can be a lifeline. Lean on them. They can provide emotional support, practical advice, and even financial assistance if needed. Don't underestimate the power of asking for help; it can be a crucial step towards your freedom.

Financial independence is another strength that cannot be ignored. If you have been managing household expenses, budgeting, or even earning an income, these skills are crucial. Financial stability can provide the foundation you need to start anew. If you are not yet financially independent, now is the time to take steps in that direction. Seek out educational opportunities, job training, or even part-time work to build your financial base.

Your self-worth has likely been eroded over time, but deep down, you know you deserve better. This intrinsic knowledge of your value is a strength that can propel you forward. Rebuilding your self-esteem will take time and effort, but it is entirely possible. Surround yourself with positive influences, engage in activities that make you feel good about yourself, and don't be afraid to seek professional help if needed.

You have already demonstrated remarkable courage by acknowledging the toxicity of your marriage. This courage is a beacon that will guide you through the difficult decisions and actions that lie ahead. Remember, the first step towards liberation is often the hardest, but it is also the most crucial.

Your strengths are not just survival mechanisms; they are the very tools that will enable you to escape and thrive. Recognize them, harness them, and let them be the driving force behind your journey to a life free from toxicity. The power to change your life is within you, and it has been all along.

Celebrating Your Successes

Amid the struggles and heartaches that accompany escaping a toxic marriage, it's easy to overlook the victories, both big and small, that mark your progress. These triumphs are not just milestones; they are testaments to your resilience, courage, and unwavering determination. Acknowledging and celebrating these successes can significantly bolster your self-esteem and keep you motivated on the path to a healthier, happier life.

Recognizing your achievements starts with a shift in perspective. Often, individuals who have endured toxic relationships are conditioned to downplay their worth and accomplishments. This mindset must change. Each step you take away from the toxicity is a powerful declaration of your strength and self-worth. Whether it's the courage to seek professional help, the resolve to set boundaries, or the bravery to finally leave, every action deserves recognition.

Create a tangible record of your successes. Write them down in a journal, create a visual board, or keep a digital log.

Seeing your progress documented can be incredibly empowering. It serves as a reminder of how far you've come and reinforces the belief that you can continue moving forward. Each entry, no matter how small it may seem, is a victory over the chains that once bound you.

Sharing your achievements with trusted friends or support groups can amplify the sense of accomplishment. These individuals can offer validation and encouragement, helping you see your progress through their eyes. Their support can be a powerful motivator, reminding you that you are not alone and that your efforts are recognized and valued.

It's also essential to reward yourself. Treat yourself to something special when you reach a significant milestone. This could be as simple as a quiet evening with your favorite book, a day trip to a place you love, or even a small gift that brings you joy. These rewards are not about materialism; they are about honoring your hard work and dedication to reclaiming your life.

Moreover, celebrating your successes fosters a positive mindset. It shifts your focus from the pain of the past to the possibilities of the future. It cultivates gratitude for your resilience and reinforces the belief in your ability to create a better life. This positive reinforcement is crucial for maintaining momentum and staying committed to your personal growth.

Incorporate rituals of celebration into your routine. This could be a monthly reflection on what you've achieved, a weekly gratitude list, or a daily affirmation of your progress. These rituals create a consistent practice of acknowledgment and appreciation, embedding a sense of accomplishment into your daily life.

Remember, every step forward, no matter how small, is a victory worth celebrating. By honoring your successes, you are not just acknowledging your progress; you are actively building a foundation of self-respect and self-love. This foundation is essential for breaking free from the shadows of a toxic marriage and stepping into the light of a new beginning.

Your journey is unique, and so are your victories. Celebrate them with the pride and joy they deserve. Each celebration is a powerful affirmation of your strength and a beacon guiding you towards a brighter, healthier future.

Chapter 13:
Cultivating Self-Compassion

Understanding Self-Compassion

Imagine living in a world where the harshest critic you face every day is yourself. Many individuals trapped in toxic marriages find themselves in this exact scenario. They internalize the negative voices and behaviors of their partners, often believing they are to blame for the dysfunction in the relationship. This relentless self-criticism erodes their self-worth and keeps them ensnared in an endless cycle of emotional pain. However, there's a powerful antidote to this self-inflicted torment: self-compassion.

Self-compassion is not about self-pity or indulging in self-centeredness. It's about treating yourself with the same kindness, understanding, and forgiveness that you would offer to a dear friend. When you extend compassion to yourself, you begin to dismantle the toxic narratives that have been imposed upon you. You start to recognize that your value is not determined by the distorted perceptions of an abusive partner. Instead, it is intrinsic and unwavering.

The first step towards cultivating self-compassion is to acknowledge your own suffering without judgment. This means recognizing that the pain you're experiencing is real and valid. It's easy to downplay your own struggles, especially when you've been conditioned to believe that your feelings are insignificant. Yet, acknowledging your pain is crucial for healing. It allows you to confront the reality of your situation and understand that your emotions are a natural response to the adversity you're facing.

Once you've acknowledged your suffering, the next step is to practice self-kindness. This involves treating yourself with the same gentleness and care that you would show to someone you love. Replace the harsh inner dialogue with words of encouragement and support. Remind yourself that it's okay to make mistakes and that you deserve patience and understanding. This shift in mindset can be transformative, as it helps to rebuild your self-esteem and fosters a sense of inner peace.

Another essential component of self-compassion is recognizing your common humanity. Understand that suffering and imperfection are part of the human experience. You are not alone in your struggles; countless others have faced similar challenges and have found a way to overcome them. This realization can provide a sense of solidarity and reduce feelings of isolation. It reminds you that no one is perfect, and everyone is deserving of compassion, including yourself.

Mindfulness is also a critical aspect of self-compassion. It involves being present in the moment and observing your thoughts and feelings without judgment. Mindfulness allows you to detach from the negative narratives that have been ingrained in your mind. By being aware of your inner experiences, you can respond to them with compassion rather than self-criticism. This practice helps to break the cycle of negative thinking and fosters a more balanced and accepting perspective.

Self-compassion is a powerful tool for breaking free from the chains of a toxic marriage. It empowers you to reclaim your self-worth and recognize that you are deserving of love and respect. By nurturing self-compassion, you can begin to heal from the emotional wounds inflicted by a toxic relationship and take the first steps towards a healthier, more fulfilling life. Embrace the journey of self-compassion, for it is the foundation upon which true liberation and happiness are built.

Practicing Self-Compassion

In the tumultuous aftermath of a toxic marriage, the road to healing often feels like a labyrinth with no clear exit. Amidst the emotional wreckage, one powerful tool stands out as a beacon of hope: self-compassion. Too often, we become our own harshest critics, allowing the echoes of our former partner's negative words to shape our self-perception. Yet, it is precisely in these moments of vulnerability that self-compassion can become our greatest ally.

Self-compassion is not about self-pity or indulging in victimhood. It is about recognizing our own humanity, acknowledging our pain without judgment, and treating ourselves with the same kindness we would extend to a dear friend. In the context of escaping a toxic marriage, this practice becomes not just beneficial, but essential. When we allow ourselves to feel compassion, we begin to dismantle the internalized criticisms that have been ingrained in us.

Consider the power of words. In a toxic marriage, words can be wielded as weapons, leaving deep emotional scars. These scars often manifest as an internal dialogue filled with self-doubt and blame. By practicing self-compassion, we actively challenge and reframe these destructive narratives. Instead of berating ourselves for perceived failures or shortcomings, we learn to speak to ourselves with gentleness and understanding. This shift in self-talk can be transformative, fostering a sense of inner peace and resilience.

Moreover, self-compassion fosters emotional resilience. In the face of adversity, it is easy to spiral into despair. However, when we approach our struggles with a compassionate mindset, we build emotional strength. We learn to see setbacks not as definitive failures, but as opportunities for growth and learning. This perspective empowers us to move forward with courage and grace, even when the path ahead is fraught with challenges.

In addition to emotional resilience, self-compassion also enhances our capacity for self-care. After enduring the turmoil of a toxic marriage, many individuals find themselves neglecting their own needs. They may feel undeserving of love and care, or simply overwhelmed by the demands of rebuilding their lives. Self-compassion reminds us that we are worthy of kindness and care, encouraging us to prioritize our well-being. This might mean setting healthy boundaries, seeking professional support, or simply allowing ourselves moments of rest and relaxation.

Furthermore, self-compassion has a profound impact on our relationships. When we treat ourselves with kindness, we set a standard for how we expect to be treated by others. We become less likely to tolerate toxic behavior and more inclined to seek out relationships that are nurturing and supportive. This shift can lead to healthier, more fulfilling connections, both with ourselves and with others.

The journey of escaping a toxic marriage is undoubtedly challenging, but self-compassion offers a powerful tool for healing and transformation. By cultivating a compassionate relationship with ourselves, we can break free from the chains of self-criticism and embrace a future filled with hope and possibility. Practicing self-compassion is not a one-time event, but a continuous, intentional effort. It is a commitment to treating ourselves with the kindness and respect that we inherently deserve, paving the way for a life of greater joy and fulfillment.

Overcoming Self-Criticism

In the throes of a toxic marriage, self-criticism often becomes a relentless companion, whispering doubts and insecurities that erode your self-worth. This internal dialogue is not just a byproduct of external negativity but a powerful force that can keep you shackled to unhappiness. Breaking free from this self-imposed prison is crucial for reclaiming your life and forging a path toward healing and empowerment.

Imagine waking up each day with a sense of purpose, unburdened by the nagging voice that questions your every move. This isn't a far-fetched dream but an attainable reality. The first step is recognizing that self-criticism is not an inherent flaw but a learned behavior, often reinforced by the toxic dynamics of your relationship. Acknowledge that these negative thoughts are not truths but distortions that can be challenged and changed.

Consider the impact of replacing self-criticism with self-compassion. Studies have shown that individuals who practice self-compassion experience lower levels of anxiety and depression. By treating yourself with the same kindness and understanding you would offer a friend, you can begin to dismantle the harmful narratives that have taken root in your mind. This shift in perspective is not about ignoring your mistakes or shortcomings but about addressing them with a balanced and forgiving mindset.

One effective strategy is to reframe your internal dialogue. When a critical thought arises, pause and question its validity. Ask yourself if you would say the same thing to someone you care about. Often, you'll find that these criticisms are harsh and unfounded. Replace them with affirmations that reflect your strengths and accomplishments. This practice may feel unnatural at first, but with consistency, it will become a powerful tool for building resilience and self-esteem.

Another crucial aspect is setting boundaries, not just with others but with yourself. Recognize when you are falling into patterns of self-criticism and consciously redirect your focus. Engage in activities that bring you joy and fulfillment, whether it's a hobby, exercise, or spending time with loved ones. These positive experiences can serve as a counterbalance to negative thoughts and reinforce a sense of self-worth.

Seeking support is also vital. Whether through therapy, support groups, or trusted friends and family, sharing your struggles can provide validation and perspective. A therapist, in particular, can offer techniques and strategies tailored to your specific needs, helping you navigate the complexities of self-criticism and its roots in your toxic marriage.

Remember, the goal is not to eradicate self-criticism entirely but to manage it in a way that it no longer dictates your self-perception and choices. By cultivating self-compassion, reframing your internal dialogue, setting boundaries, and seeking support, you can weaken the grip of self-criticism and strengthen your resolve to leave a toxic marriage.

Your journey toward freedom and self-discovery is not without challenges, but overcoming self-criticism is a pivotal step. It allows you to see yourself not through the distorted lens of negativity but as a worthy, capable individual deserving of happiness and respect. The chains of a toxic marriage may seem unbreakable, but with determination and the right tools, you can escape and build a future defined by self-love and empowerment.

Self-Compassion and Healing

A toxic marriage can leave deep scars on your soul, eroding your sense of self-worth and distorting your perception of love. It's a relentless storm that batters the very foundation of your being, leaving you feeling isolated, worthless, and broken. Yet, within this turmoil lies an opportunity for profound transformation—a chance to rebuild your life anchored in self-compassion and healing.

Self-compassion is not just a gentle pat on the back or a fleeting moment of self-indulgence. It is a powerful force that can reshape your entire being. It begins with acknowledging your pain without judgment, recognizing that your suffering is valid and real. This acknowledgment is the first step towards breaking free from the chains that have bound you. By treating yourself with the same kindness and understanding that you would offer a dear friend, you start to dismantle the internalized negativity that a toxic relationship has ingrained in you.

It's crucial to understand that self-compassion is not synonymous with self-pity. Self-pity keeps you trapped in a cycle of victimhood, whereas self-compassion empowers you to take control of your narrative. It encourages you to see beyond the immediate pain and recognize your inherent worth. This shift in perspective is transformative. It allows you to rebuild your identity on a foundation of self-respect and love, rather than the distorted image imposed by a toxic partner.

Healing from a toxic marriage is not a linear process. It's a journey that requires patience and persistence. There will be days when the shadows of the past loom large, but self-compassion provides the light to navigate through this darkness. It reminds you that healing is not about erasing the past but about integrating it into your story in a way that strengthens you. Each setback becomes an opportunity to practice forgiveness and understanding towards yourself, reinforcing your resilience and capacity for love.

Incorporating self-compassion into your daily life can be a transformative practice. Start with small acts of kindness towards yourself. This could be as simple as taking a few moments each day to breathe deeply and acknowledge your feelings, or treating yourself to a comforting activity that brings you joy. These seemingly minor actions accumulate, gradually shifting your internal dialogue from one of criticism to one of acceptance and love.

Another powerful tool in your healing arsenal is mindfulness. By staying present in the moment and observing your thoughts without judgment, you can break free from the cycle of negative thinking that a toxic marriage often perpetuates. Mindfulness helps you to identify and challenge the harmful narratives that have been imposed upon you, replacing them with a more compassionate and truthful understanding of yourself.

Surrounding yourself with a supportive community is also vital. Seek out friends, family, or support groups who understand your journey and can offer empathy and encouragement. Their presence can provide a mirror to reflect your true worth, helping you to see yourself through the eyes of love and compassion rather than criticism and disdain.

As you continue to cultivate self-compassion and embrace the healing process, you will begin to see a profound shift in your life. The chains of your toxic marriage will loosen, and you will emerge stronger, more resilient, and deeply connected to your true self. This transformation is not just about surviving but thriving, reclaiming your life with a newfound sense of purpose and joy.

Self-Compassion in Daily Life

Imagine waking up every morning with a sense of peace, knowing that you are enough just as you are. This isn't a fantasy or an unattainable dream; it is the reality you can create through the practice of self-compassion. In the throes of a toxic marriage, it's easy to lose sight of your worth and to internalize the negativity that surrounds you. However, self-compassion offers a lifeline, a way to reclaim your sense of self and heal from the emotional scars.

Self-compassion involves treating yourself with the same kindness and understanding that you would extend to a close friend. When you make a mistake or face a setback, instead of berating yourself, you offer words of encouragement and support. This approach might feel foreign at first, especially if you've been subjected to constant criticism and blame. But the power of self-compassion is transformative; it shifts your inner dialogue from one of condemnation to one of acceptance.

Consider the impact of starting your day with a few moments of self-reflection. Instead of immediately diving into the chaos, take a moment to acknowledge your feelings. Are you anxious? Overwhelmed? Sad? Recognizing these emotions without judgment is the first step in practicing self-compassion. It allows you to address your needs rather than suppress them, fostering a healthier emotional state.

Throughout the day, it's crucial to integrate small acts of kindness towards yourself. This could be as simple as taking a short break when you're feeling overwhelmed, or engaging in an activity that brings you joy. These moments of self-care are not selfish; they are necessary for your well-being. By prioritizing your own needs, you are better equipped to handle the challenges that come your way.

In a toxic marriage, criticism and negativity can erode your self-esteem. To counteract this, create a mental list of your strengths and achievements. Reflect on these regularly to remind yourself of your worth. When negative thoughts arise, challenge them by focusing on your positive attributes. This shift in perspective can gradually rebuild your confidence and sense of self.

Another powerful aspect of self-compassion is learning to forgive yourself. Everyone makes mistakes, and it's important to recognize that these do not define your entire being. Holding onto guilt and shame only perpetuates a cycle of self-loathing. Instead, acknowledge your mistakes, learn from them, and move forward with a renewed sense of purpose.

Surrounding yourself with supportive and compassionate people can also reinforce your practice of self-compassion. Seek out friends and family members who uplift and encourage you. Their positive influence can serve as a reminder that you are deserving of love and kindness.

Furthermore, mindfulness practices such as meditation or deep-breathing exercises can enhance your ability to stay present and compassionate towards yourself. These practices help quiet the mind and reduce the influence of negative, self-critical thoughts. They create a space for you to connect with your inner self and foster a sense of inner peace.

Incorporating self-compassion into your daily life is not an overnight process. It requires patience and persistence, but the rewards are profound. As you cultivate this practice, you'll find that you are more resilient, more confident, and more capable of breaking free from the chains of a toxic marriage. You deserve to live a life filled with love, respect, and compassion, starting with how you treat yourself.

Chapter 14:
Building a Supportive Community

The Importance of a Support Network

No one should endure the suffocating grip of a toxic marriage alone. The emotional and psychological toll it takes can be overwhelming, leaving you feeling isolated and powerless. Yet, the path to freedom and healing is not one you must walk in solitude. A robust support network can be your lifeline, offering the strength and encouragement you need to break free and reclaim your life.

Imagine being surrounded by people who genuinely care about your well-being, who listen without judgment, and who provide practical assistance when you need it most. This network of friends, family, and professionals can be your anchor, offering stability and perspective as you navigate the complexities of leaving a toxic relationship. Their collective wisdom and experience can illuminate your path, helping you see options and possibilities that may have seemed out of reach.

The emotional support provided by a close-knit circle of loved ones cannot be overstated. Friends and family can offer a listening ear, a shoulder to cry on, and words of encouragement that can lift your spirits during the darkest times. Their belief in you can bolster your self-esteem and remind you of your worth, counteracting the negative messages you may have internalized from your toxic partner. This emotional reinforcement is crucial for maintaining your mental health and resilience as you take steps toward independence.

Beyond emotional support, a strong network can provide practical assistance that can make a significant difference in your journey. Whether it's offering a temporary place to stay, helping with childcare, or providing financial support, these tangible acts of kindness can alleviate some of the immediate pressures you face. Knowing that you have a safety net can empower you to make decisions that prioritize your well-being without the paralyzing fear of being left with nothing.

Professional support is another vital component of your network. Therapists, counselors, and support groups can offer specialized guidance and strategies for coping with the unique challenges of leaving a toxic marriage. These professionals can help you process your experiences, develop healthy coping mechanisms, and create a concrete plan for moving forward. Legal advisors and domestic violence advocates can also provide crucial information and resources to ensure your safety and protect your rights.

A support network extends beyond just those who are physically close to you. Online communities and forums can offer a sense of solidarity and understanding, connecting you with others who have faced similar struggles. These virtual spaces can be a source of inspiration and practical advice, reinforcing the idea that you are not alone in your fight for freedom.

The importance of a support network cannot be underestimated. It provides the emotional, practical, and professional resources that are essential for breaking free from the chains of a toxic marriage. Surrounding yourself with a diverse and reliable support system can make the seemingly impossible task of leaving a harmful relationship not only achievable but also transformative. By leaning on those who care about you and seeking out professional guidance, you can find the strength and clarity needed to reclaim your life and build a future filled with hope and possibility.

Building Your Tribe

In the aftermath of a toxic marriage, isolation can feel like a heavy shroud, suffocating and relentless. But you don't have to navigate this treacherous terrain alone. The power of community and support is transformative and essential for your healing journey. Building a tribe of trusted individuals who uplift and empower you is a crucial step towards reclaiming your life and fortifying your resilience.

First, it's vital to recognize the importance of surrounding yourself with positive influences. Toxic relationships often erode self-esteem and create a distorted sense of normalcy. By connecting with those who genuinely care for your well-being, you begin to rebuild your self-worth and gain a clearer perspective on what healthy relationships look like. Seek out friends and family members who have consistently shown you love and support. Their encouragement will be a beacon of hope and a reminder that you are valued.

Moreover, consider joining support groups specifically designed for individuals recovering from toxic marriages. These groups offer a safe space to share your experiences and hear from others who have walked a similar path. The shared understanding and camaraderie found in these circles can be profoundly healing. Listening to others' stories and victories can inspire your own progress and remind you that you are not alone in this struggle.

Professional help is another cornerstone of your tribe. Therapists and counselors provide a structured environment to process your emotions and develop coping strategies. Their expertise can help you untangle the complexities of your past relationship and guide you towards healthier patterns of thinking and behavior. Don't hesitate to reach out for professional support; it is a sign of strength, not weakness.

As you build your tribe, also consider the power of online communities. Virtual forums, social media groups, and blogs dedicated to survivors of toxic marriages can be invaluable resources. These platforms allow you to connect with a broader network of individuals who understand your experience. Sharing advice, receiving feedback, and simply knowing that others are rooting for your success can be incredibly empowering.

It's equally important to set boundaries and protect your newfound support system from negative influences. Toxic individuals often have a way of seeping back into your life, undermining your progress. Be vigilant and discerning about who you allow into your inner circle. Prioritize relationships that are reciprocal and nurturing, and distance yourself from those that drain your energy or bring you down.

Lastly, remember that building a tribe is an ongoing process. Relationships evolve, and your needs may change over time. Stay open to new connections and be willing to let go of those that no longer serve your growth. Your tribe is a dynamic entity, reflecting your journey towards healing and empowerment.

The strength of your tribe lies in its diversity. Friends, family, professionals, and online allies all contribute unique perspectives and support. Together, they form a robust network that bolsters your resilience and aids in your recovery. By actively building and nurturing this tribe, you reclaim control over your life and create a foundation of love and support that empowers you to thrive beyond the shadows of a toxic marriage.

Support Groups and Resources

In the tumultuous landscape of a toxic marriage, it can often feel like you're navigating through a storm without a compass. The isolation, confusion, and emotional turmoil can be overwhelming, making it seem as though there's no safe harbor in sight. Yet, there exists a powerful lifeline that many overlook: support groups and resources specifically tailored for individuals facing the challenges of a toxic relationship.

Imagine having a circle of individuals who not only understand but have walked the same treacherous path. These support groups are not just gatherings; they are sanctuaries of empathy, wisdom, and shared strength. When you join such a group, you are not merely a participant; you become part of a community that validates your experiences and emotions. This validation is crucial because toxic relationships often erode your self-esteem, making you question your reality and worth. Hearing others articulate their struggles and victories can be profoundly healing and empowering.

Consider the transformative power of shared stories. Within these groups, narratives of endurance and recovery are exchanged, offering tangible proof that escape and healing are possible. These stories are not just anecdotes; they are blueprints for reclaiming your life. They offer practical advice, coping strategies, and, most importantly, hope. Knowing that others have successfully navigated the same treacherous waters can ignite a spark of resilience within you.

Beyond emotional support, these groups often provide invaluable resources. Expert-led sessions, workshops, and literature can equip you with the tools needed to understand the dynamics of toxic relationships and to strategize your exit. Legal advice, financial planning, and safety planning are often discussed, providing a comprehensive support system that addresses every facet of your journey. This holistic approach ensures that you are not just surviving but are empowered to rebuild your life on solid ground.

Therapists and counselors who specialize in toxic relationships can offer another layer of support. Their professional guidance can help you unravel the psychological knots that have kept you tethered to a harmful partnership. They can assist in identifying patterns of abuse, understanding your own responses, and developing healthier coping mechanisms. Therapy is not a sign of weakness; it is a powerful step towards reclaiming your mental and emotional health.

Online forums and helplines offer additional, readily accessible support. In the digital age, help is just a click away. These platforms provide anonymity and the convenience of access from anywhere, ensuring that support is available whenever you need it. They offer immediate connection to others who understand your plight, along with access to a wealth of information and resources tailored to your specific needs.

Books and articles written by survivors and experts can also serve as guiding lights. These written words can be both comforting and instructional, offering insights and strategies that have been tested by time and experience. They can serve as companions on your journey, offering wisdom and solace when you need it most.

Taking advantage of these support systems is not just an option; it is a necessity. The chains of a toxic marriage are not easily broken, but with the right support, they can be shattered. You deserve a life free from the shadows of manipulation and abuse. By reaching out and tapping into these resources, you are taking a decisive step towards reclaiming your power and your peace. The path to freedom begins with the courage to seek help and the wisdom to accept it.

Helping Others in Similar Situations

One of the most transformative actions you can take after liberating yourself from a toxic marriage is to extend a helping hand to others who find themselves ensnared in similar circumstances. The power of shared experience cannot be overstated. When you offer your insights and support to those still trapped in the throes of emotional turmoil, you become a beacon of hope and a testament to the possibility of a brighter future.

Consider the profound impact your story can have. Your experiences, no matter how painful, have endowed you with a unique perspective and an arsenal of coping strategies that can be invaluable to someone else. By sharing your journey, you validate their struggles and remind them that they are not alone. This sense of solidarity can be the catalyst they need to take those first, daunting steps toward freedom.

It's essential to remember that helping others does not only benefit them—it also fosters your own healing. The act of giving, of being there for someone else, can bring a sense of purpose and fulfillment that accelerates your emotional recovery. When you see the positive changes in someone else's life because of your support, it reaffirms your own strength and resilience. This mutual exchange of support creates a virtuous cycle of healing and empowerment.

Engaging with support groups, both in-person and online, is a practical way to start. These communities are often filled with individuals who are searching for understanding and guidance. By actively participating and sharing your story, you can offer real, tangible advice and encouragement. Your presence in these groups can also help dismantle the isolation that many victims of toxic marriages feel, creating a network of support and understanding.

Another impactful way to assist others is through mentorship. Taking someone under your wing, offering consistent support, and guiding them through their own escape can be incredibly rewarding. This one-on-one connection allows for a deeper, more personalized form of assistance. You can tailor your advice to their specific situation, providing a lifeline that is both practical and deeply empathetic.

Advocacy is another powerful avenue. Raising awareness about the signs and dangers of toxic relationships can prevent others from falling into similar traps. Whether through writing, public speaking, or social media, your voice can reach a wide audience. Sharing educational resources, personal anecdotes, and actionable advice can empower others to recognize and escape their own toxic situations.

Volunteering with organizations dedicated to supporting victims of domestic abuse and toxic relationships can also be incredibly impactful. These organizations often provide critical resources such as legal assistance, counseling, and safe housing. Your firsthand experience can enhance the support they offer, making it more relatable and effective.

Helping others in similar situations is more than just an act of kindness—it's a powerful affirmation of your own journey and resilience. It's about creating a ripple effect of empowerment and change. By stepping into the role of a supporter, mentor, or advocate, you contribute to a larger movement towards healing and liberation. Your story, your strength, and your willingness to help can transform lives, just as your own life has been transformed. This is not just an opportunity; it's a responsibility that carries the potential to create a world where fewer people have to suffer in silence and more can step into the light of freedom and self-worth.

Creating a Safe Space

In the turbulent waves of a toxic marriage, finding a sanctuary becomes crucial. A safe space isn't merely a physical location; it's a mental refuge where one can breathe freely, think clearly, and regain strength. Establishing this sanctuary is a transformative step towards reclaiming your life and sanity.

The first step in creating a safe space is acknowledging your need for one. Denial is a common defense mechanism in toxic relationships, but confronting the reality of your situation is essential. Accepting that you deserve peace and security is the foundation upon which you will build your sanctuary. This acknowledgment empowers you to take deliberate actions towards safeguarding your well-being.

Next, consider the physical environment. Identify a place where you feel most comfortable and secure. It could be a room in your home, a friend's house, or even a quiet spot in a nearby park. The key is to choose a location where you can retreat without fear of intrusion or judgment. Make this space your own by adding elements that bring you comfort and joy—be it soft lighting, soothing music, or cherished mementos.

Creating emotional boundaries is equally important. In a toxic marriage, emotional manipulation and control are often rampant. Establishing clear boundaries helps protect your mental health. Communicate your limits assertively and consistently. It may be challenging at first, but standing firm in your boundaries is a vital act of self-respect and self-preservation.

Support systems play a critical role in maintaining your safe space. Surround yourself with individuals who uplift and support you. Friends, family, or support groups can provide a listening ear, practical advice, and emotional strength. Sharing your experiences with others who understand your plight can be incredibly validating and empowering. Don't hesitate to seek professional help if needed; therapists and counselors can offer valuable tools and strategies to navigate your circumstances.

Engaging in self-care practices fortifies your safe space. Self-care isn't a luxury; it's a necessity. Regularly engage in activities that nourish your body, mind, and spirit. Exercise, meditation, hobbies, and adequate rest are crucial components of a healthy routine. These practices not only enhance your well-being but also reinforce your resolve to maintain your safe space.

Mindfulness and self-reflection are powerful tools in this process. Take time to reflect on your thoughts and emotions without judgment. Journaling can be an effective way to process your feelings and track your progress. Mindfulness practices, such as meditation or deep breathing exercises, help center your mind and reduce stress. These practices enable you to stay grounded and focused, even amidst chaos.

Empowerment is the ultimate goal of creating a safe space. This sanctuary is not a place to hide but a foundation from which you can rebuild your strength and confidence. As you establish and nurture your safe space, you will find your inner voice growing stronger. This inner strength will guide you in making decisions that align with your best interests and lead you towards a healthier, more fulfilling life.

Creating a safe space is a courageous and empowering step towards breaking free from the chains of a toxic marriage. It's a declaration of your worth and a commitment to your well-being. By cultivating this sanctuary, you reclaim your power and pave the way for a brighter, healthier future.

Chapter 15:
Embracing Your New Life

Celebrating Your Journey

Imagine waking up each day with a renewed sense of freedom, where the air feels lighter and every moment brims with possibilities. This is the life that awaits you once you break free from a toxic marriage. It is not merely about leaving behind the pain and suffering; it's about stepping into a world where your happiness, well-being, and dreams are the primary focus.

Your decision to leave a toxic marriage is a monumental step, one that requires immense courage and determination. However, it's crucial to recognize that this choice is a testament to your strength and self-worth. You have chosen to prioritize your mental and emotional health over the chains that once bound you. This is not just an escape; it is a declaration of your right to live a life filled with love, respect, and joy.

As you transition into this new chapter, take a moment to acknowledge the progress you have made. Each step forward, no matter how small, is a victory. Celebrate the resilience that has carried you through the darkest times and the wisdom that has guided you toward a brighter future. These achievements, though sometimes overlooked, are the building blocks of your newfound independence.

It is essential to surround yourself with positive influences that reinforce your decision and support your growth. Seek out friends, family, or support groups who understand your journey and can offer encouragement and advice. Their presence will remind you that you are not alone and that your choice to leave was not only valid but necessary.

Reclaiming your identity is a pivotal part of this transformation. In a toxic marriage, it is easy to lose sight of who you are and what you desire. Take this opportunity to rediscover your passions, hobbies, and goals. Engage in activities that bring you joy and fulfillment. Whether it's picking up an old hobby or exploring new interests, these pursuits will help you reconnect with yourself and rebuild your confidence.

Financial independence is another critical aspect to consider. Ensuring that you have the means to support yourself is empowering and liberating. Take control of your finances, create a budget, and seek professional advice if needed. This autonomy will not only provide you with security but also reinforce your ability to thrive on your own.

Emotional healing is a journey that requires patience and self-compassion. Allow yourself to feel and process the emotions that arise during this time. Therapy or counseling can be invaluable in helping you navigate these feelings and develop healthy coping mechanisms. Remember, healing is not linear, and it's okay to have setbacks. What matters is your commitment to your well-being and your willingness to seek help when needed.

Your future is a blank canvas, waiting for you to paint it with the colors of your choosing. Embrace this opportunity to create a life that reflects your true self. Set goals that excite and challenge you, and take deliberate steps toward achieving them. The freedom you now have is a powerful tool; use it to build a life that not only meets your needs but also nurtures your soul.

In this newfound freedom, there lies an incredible potential for growth and happiness. By leaving behind a toxic marriage, you have already proven your strength and resilience. Now, it's time to harness that power and create a life that celebrates your worth and potential. This is your moment to shine, to live authentically, and to embrace the happiness that you so rightfully deserve.

Living in the Present

Imagine waking up each day with a sense of liberation, unburdened by the shadows of a toxic marriage. This is not just an abstract ideal but a tangible reality within reach. The key lies in the present moment, a sanctuary that offers solace and renewal. You might wonder, why is living in the present so crucial? The answer is simple yet profound: it is the only moment you truly possess. The past is a memory, the future a projection; only the present is real and actionable.

When you are entangled in a toxic marriage, your mind often oscillates between past regrets and future anxieties. These mental excursions drain your energy and cloud your judgment. By focusing on the here and now, you reclaim your power. You can make choices that align with your well-being and start to rebuild your life, one mindful decision at a time.

Living in the present is not about ignoring the past or neglecting future plans. It's about grounding yourself in the current moment to make more conscious, empowered choices. Imagine the clarity and strength that come from being fully aware of your thoughts, emotions, and surroundings. This heightened awareness allows you to break free from the mental chains that a toxic relationship imposes.

Mindfulness is a powerful tool in this transformation. By practicing mindfulness, you train your mind to stay anchored in the present. Simple exercises like deep breathing, meditation, or even mindful walking can shift your focus from the turmoil of a toxic relationship to the tranquility of the present. These practices help you observe your thoughts and emotions without judgment, creating a mental space where you can process your experiences more objectively.

Consider the impact of this shift on your daily life. Instead of reacting impulsively to triggers, you respond thoughtfully. You start to notice the small joys and opportunities that each day brings. This change in perspective can be incredibly empowering. It allows you to see the possibilities for happiness and fulfillment that exist outside the confines of a toxic marriage.

Furthermore, living in the present fosters resilience. It equips you with the mental fortitude to face challenges head-on without being overwhelmed by them. When you are present, you are more adaptable and resourceful. You can navigate the complexities of leaving a toxic marriage with greater confidence and less fear.

The benefits extend beyond your mental and emotional well-being. When you live in the present, you are more attuned to your physical needs as well. You become more conscious of how your body feels and what it needs to heal and thrive. This holistic approach to well-being strengthens your resolve and enhances your overall quality of life.

Living in the present also improves your relationships with others. As you become more centered and balanced, you attract positive, nurturing relationships. You are better equipped to set healthy boundaries and communicate effectively, fostering connections built on mutual respect and understanding.

In essence, living in the present is a radical act of self-love and empowerment. It is a declaration that you deserve to experience life fully, free from the toxic patterns of the past. By grounding yourself in the present, you pave the way for a future filled with hope, joy, and endless possibilities. Seize this moment, and let it be the foundation upon which you build your new, liberated life.

Planning for the Future

As you stand on the threshold of a new life, it's essential to shift your focus from the past to the horizon that stretches ahead. The scars of a toxic marriage are profound, but they do not define your future. They are merely chapters in a story that is still being written. Your future holds infinite possibilities, and now is the time to plan for it with intention and clarity.

First and foremost, financial independence is crucial. Begin by assessing your current financial situation. Create a budget that reflects your new reality, prioritizing essential expenses while setting aside funds for emergencies. Seek professional advice, if necessary, to ensure you make informed decisions about savings, investments, and potential career opportunities. Financial stability is not just about money; it's about reclaiming control over your life and your future.

Next, consider your personal and professional goals. What dreams have you shelved because of the constraints of your marriage? Dust them off, and give them the attention they deserve. Whether it's going back to school, starting a new career, or pursuing a passion project, now is the time to invest in yourself. Set realistic, achievable goals and break them down into manageable steps. Celebrate each milestone, no matter how small, because each one brings you closer to the life you envision.

Building a support network is another critical aspect of planning for the future. Surround yourself with people who uplift and encourage you. Seek out friends, family, and support groups who understand your journey and can offer guidance and empathy. Professional counseling can also be a valuable resource, providing a safe space to process your emotions and develop strategies for moving forward. Remember, you don't have to navigate this path alone; there are people who care and want to see you succeed.

Emotional healing is a gradual process, and it's important to be patient with yourself. Practice self-care regularly, prioritizing activities that nurture your mind, body, and spirit. Meditation, exercise, journaling, and creative pursuits can all contribute to your overall well-being. As you heal, you'll find that your capacity for joy and fulfillment expands, allowing you to embrace new experiences with an open heart.

Consider also the impact of your decisions on any children involved. Their well-being is paramount, and they too will need support and reassurance. Open, honest communication is key, as is creating a stable, loving environment for them. Professional guidance, such as family therapy, can be invaluable in helping them process the changes and adjust to the new dynamics.

Finally, cultivate a mindset of resilience and optimism. Challenges will arise, but they are not insurmountable. Each obstacle is an opportunity to grow stronger and more self-reliant. Focus on what you can control, and let go of what you cannot. Visualize the life you want to lead, and take proactive steps toward making it a reality. Your future is not a distant dream; it is a tangible goal that you can achieve with determination and perseverance.

By planning for the future with intentionality and hope, you are not just escaping the chains of a toxic marriage; you are forging a new path of empowerment and freedom. The best is yet to come, and it starts with the steps you take today.

Achieving Personal Growth

Leaving a toxic marriage is a monumental step. It's a decision that signifies not just the end of a painful chapter but the beginning of a transformative phase in your life. The path ahead may seem daunting, but it is also brimming with untapped potential for personal growth. This is not merely about surviving; it's about thriving, evolving into a stronger, more resilient version of yourself.

Imagine shedding the layers of self-doubt and fear that have accumulated over the years. Picture yourself reclaiming your identity, one that has been overshadowed by the toxicity of your relationship. This is your opportunity to rediscover who you are and what you truly want from life. The first step in this process is recognizing that you deserve better. Your well-being, happiness, and mental health are paramount. Allow yourself to believe that you are worthy of love and respect, starting with the love and respect you give yourself.

Personal growth begins with self-awareness. Reflect on the experiences that have shaped you, both good and bad. Understand the patterns that led you to a toxic relationship and recognize the strength it took to leave. This introspection is not about assigning blame but about gaining insight. It's about understanding your boundaries and learning to protect them fiercely in the future.

Next, focus on setting realistic and empowering goals. These goals should be about nurturing yourself, both physically and emotionally. Whether it's pursuing a hobby you've always been passionate about, furthering your education, or simply dedicating time each day to self-care, these actions are crucial. They serve as reminders that your happiness and fulfillment are within your control.

Surround yourself with positive influences. Seek out friends, family, and communities that uplift and support you. Their encouragement can be a powerful catalyst for change. Engage with others who have walked a similar path and emerged stronger. Their stories can offer hope and strategies that you might not have considered. Remember, you are not alone, and there is strength in solidarity.

Therapy can be an invaluable resource in this journey. A professional can help you navigate the complex emotions and traumas associated with leaving a toxic marriage. They can provide tools and techniques to build resilience and foster a healthier mindset. Don't hesitate to reach out for this support; it is a sign of strength, not weakness.

As you progress, celebrate your victories, no matter how small they may seem. Each step forward is a testament to your courage and determination. Acknowledge the progress you make, and use it as motivation to keep moving forward. Personal growth is not a destination but a continuous process. There will be setbacks, but each challenge you overcome will fortify your resolve and enhance your growth.

Reclaiming your life after a toxic marriage is a powerful act of self-love. It's an affirmation that you refuse to be defined by past pain. By focusing on personal growth, you are choosing to invest in yourself, to prioritize your happiness and well-being. This decision will not only transform your life but also inspire others who find themselves in similar situations. So, take that courageous step forward and embrace the boundless potential that lies ahead. Your future is yours to shape, and it starts with the commitment to grow.

Maintaining Your Progress

In the aftermath of liberating yourself from a toxic marriage, the euphoria of newfound freedom can be intoxicating. However, the path to sustained liberation requires vigilance and conscious effort. The initial steps you've taken are monumental, but to ensure lasting peace and growth, a continuous commitment to maintaining your progress is essential.

First and foremost, establishing a robust support system is crucial. Surround yourself with individuals who genuinely understand and respect your journey. These could be friends, family members, or support groups who can offer emotional reinforcement and practical advice. Their encouragement and understanding will serve as a bulwark against moments of doubt or temptation to revert to old patterns.

Engaging in regular self-reflection is another cornerstone of maintaining progress. Allocate time each week to assess your emotional and mental state. Journaling can be an effective method for this. By documenting your thoughts, feelings, and experiences, you create a tangible record of your growth and identify areas that may need more attention. This practice not only keeps you accountable but also reinforces your commitment to personal development.

Setting and pursuing new goals is vital. The dissolution of a toxic marriage often leaves a void that needs to be filled with constructive and fulfilling activities. Whether it's advancing your career, picking up a new hobby, or dedicating time to personal fitness, these goals provide a sense of purpose and direction. They act as positive distractions, steering you away from any lingering negativity associated with your past relationship.

Therapy or counseling shouldn't be overlooked. Professional guidance can offer profound insights and coping strategies tailored to your specific circumstances. Therapists can help you navigate complex emotions and traumas that may still linger, ensuring that you don't inadvertently carry old wounds into new relationships or aspects of your life.

Mindfulness and meditation practices can also play a significant role in maintaining your progress. These techniques help in grounding yourself in the present moment, reducing stress, and fostering a sense of inner peace. Regular meditation can enhance emotional regulation, making it easier to respond thoughtfully rather than react impulsively to challenging situations.

Another essential aspect is setting healthy boundaries. In the wake of a toxic marriage, it's imperative to redefine what you will and will not tolerate in your interactions with others. Clear boundaries protect your emotional well-being and prevent the intrusion of negative influences. Communicate these boundaries assertively and consistently, ensuring that they're respected by those around you.

Physical health should not be neglected. Regular exercise, a balanced diet, and sufficient sleep are fundamental to overall well-being. Physical activity, in particular, has been shown to improve mood and reduce anxiety, which can be incredibly beneficial as you adjust to your new life.

Lastly, celebrate your successes, no matter how small they may seem. Acknowledge and reward yourself for the strides you've made. This positive reinforcement helps to build self-esteem and reinforces the belief that you are capable of sustaining this new, healthier chapter of your life.

Maintaining your progress is an ongoing process, one that requires dedication and self-compassion. By actively nurturing your mental, emotional, and physical health, you fortify the foundation of your newfound freedom, ensuring that the chains of your past remain firmly broken.

www.ingramcontent.com/pod-product-compliance
Lightning Source LLC
LaVergne TN
LVHW041220080526
838199LV00082B/1322